A NEW BLUEPRINT FOR MARRIAGE

by MERRILY NEILL
and
JOANNE TANGEDAHL

Illustrated by John Hyde
Photograph by Sue Permenter

For information contact:
Coleman Graphics, 99 Milbar Boulevard, Farmingdale, N.Y. 11735

A New Blueprint For Marriage

I dedicate ...

Without the existence, support and encouragement, plus huge amounts of child care from my Reconnected mate, this book would not have been possible, from any perspective. I, therefore, dedicate this book to Jim Neill and to all of the facets of myself I enjoy sharing with him.

Merrily

I dedicate this book to the relationships of my life -- some from childhood, my marriage, my lovely seven children and their loves, my supportive and accepting friends, my clients, and my special relationships. They taught me the importance of separation and connection, the very essence of life.

Joanne

TABLE OF CONTENTS

I
PERSPECTIVE

She watches him as he picks up the old brown suitcase he's thrown some clothes into and she casually wonders why he put in that blue shirt he'd never liked. As she stands there, silent, almost not breathing, she watches him gather all his shaving gear and leave the bedroom. She follows him and feels as if she's watching two strangers in an unknown play. In a last minute impulsive gesture, he grabs the old green lamp Aunt Sarah gave them and shoves it under his free arm. He struggles out the front door, his hair uncombed, his face white. She vaguely thinks to herself, "Who are we? What's happening to us? How did this go so wrong?" She feels numb. The screen door slams and he's gone.

This couple, like couples everywhere, are experiencing the impact of the crisis in marriage today, a crisis caused by the attempt to continue using the old-fashioned pattern of marriage that worked for past generations, but not now.

Marriage has been regarded as an end in itself, a product, a state to be achieved. Marriage is not a product. Marriage is a process. To guide couples through this process, we provide a blueprint, a guideline for moving from one stage of the process to the next, a design for building and rebuilding a marriage.

Yet this crisis we are experiencing in marriage contains an element of opportunity; it is not a break**down** so much as a break**through.** The crisis appears in each new statistical report showing divorce rates increasing. Presently, one out of every two marriages terminates in divorce. Now, couples have the opportunity to create a new pattern.

However, couples face future shock. New innovations come about even before adjustments have been made to present changes, and the marriage relationship is no exception. We human beings have changed and matured, therefore the marriage relationship must alter to function successfully.

The momentus growth and change that permeated the 20th century affected every area of life. The list of influences on marriage includes the Industrial Revolution, Women's Liberation, advances in communication, knowledge and technology and the diminished power of religion. The old ideals about marriage crumbled under the weight of these new developments.

The old-fashioned ideal contained an emotionally and financially dependent wife, a heirarchy of power where the husband was boss, loss of individual identity, and rigid rules and regulations prescribed by church and society. Guilt and blaming were the tools that insured compliance. Partners encouraged and wanted their spouse to be dependent on them. The feelings of security helped each feel connected with the world and humanity through the partner.

The rules, standards, values, roles and ideals appropriate for the past focused the couple's energy on survival needs. Time and energy were not available to devote to intimacy and identity needs, and choices about everything were few.

To experience marriage as an institution implies prescribed and rigid rules and no choices; to experience marriage as a process implies decision-making, choosing at every step. Our **New Blueprint for Marriage** traces marriage through five progressive stages of growth, allowing choices at every stage to create each marriage as a unique relationship.

A blueprint is a guide or pattern for building a structure and our **New Blueprint for Marriage** offers a guide through the process of building a marriage. The five stages are Happiness Bubble, Bursting the Bubble, Self-Discovery, Bridge Building and Reconnection. Each stage is necessary, providing an essential element to the process.

How does this differ from our past view of marriage? The new ideal contains the opportunity for independence within the marriage, equality of power, individuality, and freedom of choice. Acceptance and responsibility are the tools that insure cooperation.

Our definition of marriage, broader than the mere legal term, is a loving, sharing relationship between two people who are attempting to live responsibly together, with the welfare of both taken into consideration ... with a commitment toward the future.

This broader definition includes couples living together with or without benefit of legal or church sanction, homosexual couples, and couples separated for emotional or logistical reasons. The marriage as described is regarded as an emotional, spiritual commitment.

Marriage is here to stay and **A New Blueprint for Marriage** provides guidance to create a marriage that works.

II
OVERVIEW OF THE MODEL

Most theorists agree that human beings are in a process of growth, i.e., moving from one stage in their development on to another. To satisfactorily move through this process, it is extremely helpful to understand the steps, to know where you are in the process, or to be able to see an overview of the situation. People are able to deal more effectively with any process and to eliminate the blocks to understanding when they have an overall picture of the entire process involved.

For this reson, we are presenting our model of the stages in a marital relationship so that you can use this knowledge as a frame of reference for you to evaluate your marital situation, find out where you are in the process, understand the dynamics of each stage and have techniques appropriate for more effective growth for your marriage.

A marriage is a process with five definable stages in the growth of the relationship: the Happiness Bubble, Bursting the Bubble, Self-Discovery, Bridge Building and Reconnection. All of the stages are important in the process. Necessary aspects are developed as progress is made through each of them.

Often one or more of the stages becomes labeled as bad. This is not so! Just as in constructing a house, you would not skip laying the foundation, in marriage, there will be more stability if all stages are experienced.

Difficulty is encountered when the couple becomes locked into one of the stages and the growth of the relationship becomes blocked. The natural tendency toward growth exerts tremendous pressure on the relationship at this point and trouble ensues. Most often, at this time, one of the partners will look at their spouse and say, "If only she (or he) would change, everything would be so much better." They are unable to see themselves and the part they are playing in the blockage. It is easier to see what the partner is doing. Unable to see what is actually happening, they are truly stuck.

Does marriage produce a feeling of completeness, an identification at last, new and better feelings and continued happiness? No, marriage can be an experience that is most rewarding but it is not a panacea. Problems to be resolved continue to arise. The spouses are human beings, not perfect, with individual and often conflicting needs, feelings and desires. They each have a way of viewing the world derived from their own family of origin and their unique life experience that is different from the view of their spouse. Each has hopes, dreams and aspirations that are unique. Marriage of these two people presents many satisfactions and joys but many problems too. Spouses who do not understand this fact then want to run, to escape into separation or divorce as soon as they discover their hopes and dreams are not being actualized and that there are differences to be resolved.

There is a better way. We can (1) accept that marriage is not perfect, (2) neither are the people involved, (3) learn the overall process of a satisfactory marriage, (4) take charge of the relationship and (5) learn how to comfortably be together. The end result is feeling satisfied and fulfilled with a real, live, unfolding marriage that has its ups and downs. There are tremendous rewards in a loving, sharing relationship and they are worth the effort it takes to achieve them. Seeing the overall picture presented in this book will provide information that will move the marriage on to new and more satisfying levels.

The first stage, entitled the Happiness Bubble is full of fantasy. One's hopes and dreams are about this relationship and what it will be, about the spouse and how perfect this person is. Dreams of a perfectly fantastic future fill the mind of each of them. They feel happy, fulfilled and satisfied. They are truly married to The Prince or The Princess of their dreams and this person is on a pedestal being adored.

Each has his own unique fantasy dancing through his or her head. They think it is reality and that their partner feels the same way, unaware that the fantasy in the partner's mind is entirely different from their own. They are guessing, assuming and reading the mind of the partner.

Denial is ever present and necessary to maintain this fantasy that the partner and the relationship is perfect. Internally, almost unaware, each partner is saying to the other partner, "Only let me hear what I want to hear and see what I want to see." The maintenance of the fantasy is of prime concern and all energy is directed to achieving this end. All the anger and disappointment is denied, carefully buried out of awareness. After all Princes and Princesses don't do such ordinary things as needing a bath or being inconsiderate of others.

The couple learns patterns of effectively manipulating each other in order to obtain a match for their fantasy and to keep the Happiness Bubble intact. Rituals develop in the relationship that provide the couple with a feeling of safety and security.

The positive aspect of this stage is that we never progress without a dream. Couples need a comfortable period to be together in order to build a solid base, to build a desire to stay together. They need this time to experience the possible payoff in a loving, sharing relationship.

The problem encountered at this point is that the focus has been only on particular aspects of the marriage or the partner. This narrow focus is limiting. All parts need to be viewed or the picture is incomplete. We need all parts of ourselves to function as a whole, fulfilled human being and if we deny certain aspects of ourselves, we end up a distortion of our real selves.

Marriages are formed with the unspoken understanding that we will maintain this fantasy. We will not go beyond this bubble. We will be everything to each other. We will fulfill each other's dreams. This stage can be maintained indefinitely, as long as both people live up to their partner's expectations. Some marriages stay here for 20 years or always. What a difficult contract to enforce.

The second stage is Bursting the Bubble. Here the denial is falling away and the couple is faced with the loss of the fantasy. They are disillusioned with their partner, with their marriage and with themselves. Anger, rather than denial, characterize this stage. The power struggle is overt now and moves out into fights with each other. Each struggles for the marriage to proceed along the lines that he or she had envisioned it. The battle to maintain their own fantasy is out in the open.

This battle is different for each couple because

every person brings into the marriage his or her own weapons, methods for coping with life, learned as a child. Sometimes, it is loud anger and fighting, or it may be withdrawing, sulking or depression. It may be crying and self-pity displays. It may be physical illness. It could be seductive sexual ploys, or withholding, passive stances. Whatever method or combination of methods we choose to use, the purpose is the same -- to control the spouse.

Underneath all of this anger, there is tremendous grieving, a grieving over the loss of the dream, the fantasy. When one finally opens his or her eyes and looks at reality and finds it different from the fantasy, the grief is inevitable, natural and necessary. It has to be experienced to move on the next phases in the marriage. How sad that the world is not like our dreams.

Dependency on the partner to make the world complete is very much a part of these first two stages. It is as if there are two halves that make up one whole instead of two whole people sharing a relationship. This dependency breeds anger.

After being angry enemies, a new thought begins to dawn gradually. It says, "Well, if my partner can't meet all of my needs, I don't have to be angry, I'll just do it myself." Even though the Bursting of the Bubble is painful, this realization that the individual not only can but must meet his or her **own** needs is often a relief. It answers the question, "If my partner cannot meet my needs, then who can? ME! I'll do it myself." With this, the move has been made into the third stage, Self-Discovery.

The growth taking place in this stage can be a struggle but it is often looked back upon as a most rewarding period. In some cases, by the third stage the individuals may not be living together or even married any longer. If they are still married, behavior in this Self-Discovery stage may be changing careers, having an affair, taking a self-improvement course, or spending money on one's self. The partner often will resist this change because it is an unfamiliar wave in the equilibrium which reinforces the fear that the partner will leave, maybe forever, showing lack of love.

The personal conflict of the Self-Discovery stage is represented in the struggle between "What I think of myself vs what others think of me -- especially my spouse." The task of the partners here is to learn about themselves, not as a partnership but as individuals entering a partnership. Until you know who you are and how to present yourself, your partner does not and cannot really know who you are.

To reiterate, the steps take this order: (1) find out who you are, (2) find out what you want your partner to know about you, and then (3) share this so your spouse can grow to know you. With this, effective relating becomes possible.

The problem with getting to know yourself is that there are facets of you that you may not like and now you will have to admit they exist. However, there are also corollary strong parts of you that you must be willing to claim as your own. Knowing yourself includes recognizing both the negative and positive, both the strong and weak parts. This is the way **real** people are.

The goal of thc Self-Discovery stage is to know yourself well enough to choose what to give or not give to yourself, therefore fulfilling you as a person so that, in turn, you will have something to give to someone else -- especially a partner. Giving then becomes free from strings and shows the independence of each person, thereby benefiting the relationship as a whole.

The work to discover yourself pays off in the marriage in the next stage called Bridge Building. A new bridge must be built to your partner, a brick at a time, because now there are two new self-knowledgeable people, each choosing whether or not to remain in the marriage. Each individual need not be perfect and the Bridge Building phase requires your partner to accept your less-than-perfect self. The sentence characterizing this stage is, "If you don't like me the way I am, you can get out."

Trust is beginning to build as the negotiators, you and your partner, are presenting your real selves. It is far easier to trust a person who will admit a weakness than insist on perfection. A bonus for each person is the freedom from the fear that the other person will discover a flaw, an imperfect surprise aspect that would ruin everything. It would only ruin a fantasy, but the fantasy is cheerfully relinquished by now.

Having faced the good and bad facets of yourself also helps you to choose how to present yourself to the public. You may find that your public and private behavior is now more alike because less of your behavior is based on the opinion of others, and you have given up trying to impress them. Your worth and value is not dependent on their approval any longer.

One young girl often kept her hand over her mouth because she was told that her laugh was too loud by her parents. As she began to accept herself, she permitted herself to laugh as loud in public as she spontaneously did in private. She stopped hiding and took her hand away from her mouth. She had learned that it is okay to laugh loud if you do not care what outsiders think about you.

So after the connections have begun during the Bridge Building, the couple is able to move on to the last stage, Reconnection. It is summarized by the statements, "You know yourself, and I know me, and we're beginning to really know each other. Now we can decide if we can stay here and allow each other the freedom to be who we are and to grow. We can choose some of the old things we want to keep that were present in our fantasy. The difference is that we are choosing, not as dependents but as independents." Each party is an adult with full knowledge of the situation. Now each has the tools and knowledge to form a marriage contract that will create the kind of relationship that both will be pleased to have.

The main characteristics of this stage are trust and freedom. The marriage contract decided upon by the parties is based on trust of the partner, freedom of choice, and knowledge of oneself and their partner.

Each stage is filled with struggle vs joy and the temptation to stay put vs the intrigue to move on. Since this is a process, one cannot just jump to the last stage, but must complete every preceding stage or the necessary ingredients discovered at one stage are not present at the end. Sunflower seeds do not bloom. Only sunflower seeds, that have grown to maturity, bloom.

Arriving at a new contract for marriage is not the end. The end is death and growth is life and a recontracted marriage offers the shelter to grow with a new-found security and warmth. Reconnection has fights and struggles as each party grows and changes. The struggles are born, however, in the security of trusting the partner to be there and to be accepting, and that they will lead to an ever more positive Reconnection.

In this book we plan to present each stage in depth, applicable psychological theory, effects of every stage on the outside world, and tools and techniques to help the marriage. To aid your use of the book, each chapter on the stages of marriage will be presented in the following format:

I. Identifying the Stages

II. Theoretical Perspectives

III. Effects of this Stage on:

- A. Sex
- B. Social situation
- C. Children and household duties
- D. Communication
- E. Work and play
- F. Self-concept

IV. Techniques and Tools

- A. How to find the feelings and fears
- B. How to change your attitude
- C. How to change your behavior
- D. How to deal with staying in a stage by choice
- E. How to work with an unwilling partner
- F. How to work with a willing partner

If you want information on a specific issue in a marriage relationship, i.e., how these stages affect children, look in each chapter for the sub-sections labeled children.

When people have a job, they put out a great deal of effort to understand what is required of them to be successful. Yet those same people feel that once they are married, they can relax and all will be well. That is no more true in marriage than it is in a work situation. Continued interest, care and effort insure continued success.

JH

III
FEELINGS

Feelings are such a powerful force in life and yet awareness and understanding of them is limited and confused. Feeling happy and satisfied is the goal of most people. They have ideas of what they want that will make them happy. "If only he'd get home from work on time, I'd feel so much better." She feels as most people often do that some event outside herself will **make** her happy. Definitely not so! This is why she is disillusioned time after time. It is her interpretation and evaluation of the event that produces her feelings. She has not learned that happiness is a state of mind that she herself produces. Each person individually creates his or her own feeling state. It is produced in their body by their thought process. If human beings want to learn how to change from a negative feeling state to a positive one, it is necessary to have some understanding of this powerful process.

Awareness of feelings provides people with valuable information about where they are emotionally at any particular moment, about who they are today as opposed to yesterday, and about what they want and need. People require this information that is provided by feelings. Once they are aware of it they can decide what needs to be done to rectify the situation and create a more satisfactory life experience.

Feelings are energy. This energy flows through the body. Remember when you were angry and how the anger just filled you up; or remember when you were excited and the butterflies fluttered in your stomach? That was the feeling-energy that was flowing through your body bringing information about what is happening at the moment for you. This is very much like a ticker tape pumping out data from moment to moment about changes in the stock market.

Feelings are simply information, they are not good or bad. They just are. Most people were taught as they grew up that there are good feelings and bad feelings, and one certainly should not feel or express the bad feelings. "Nice children don't act like that." This is an erroneous belief.

Feelings are simply information -- information required in order to know life and possibly change it for the better. Anger communicates to oneself that something is not right and needs attention. People need to feel fear. If they did not, they might walk out in front of a Mack truck. People need to experience joy because then they know that their life situation is working well. They can become aware of what it is and put out some effort to keep it that way and continue to feel fulfilled.

Yes, awareness of feelings is needed and valuable. Feelings are energy flowing through the body bringing information. They are not good or bad. They just are.

However, many people turn off their feelings. They are taught they should not feel what they feel and as a result, they denied and blocked their true feelings from their awareness. Little girls are taught it is not lady-like to be angry. "You just look so horrid when you're angry. What will Grandma think?" Young growing males are told that "Big boys" do not cry. Today many men are not even aware of their sad feelings. They have society's permission to get an ulcer or have a heart attack instead.

Sometimes one's life situation seems too impossible to change and the pain involved is so devastating that the only option apparent to a person is to deny and repress feelings for a time. Otherwise they might feel overwhelmed. So for a time the most effective and appropriate thing is to deny and block the feelings. "Oh, I'm not mad." However, if this is continued, problems begin because the information needed is not available for the person and the energy is locked in the body. It usually is an underlying fear that is the basis for such a blockage. This fear may be covered by other feelings because we experience many feelings at one time.

The layers of feelings may unfold such as this;

A husband's spouse decides she wants to go to work. He responds with indifference seeming not to care at all. She is confused by this because earlier he had been so supportive of her decision. He may possibly be allowing the safest feeling to manifest because he may be feeling angry. He might think to himself, "Now I have to start supper and if she really loved me she'd be here taking care of me." He knows this feeling is irrational, unrealistic and childish so he hides it under indifference. He has not yet learned that all feelings are good and need to be listened to. However, under this anger is resentment because he wanted to be cared for and his mother always demonstrated her love through meal preparation which naturally led to the husband's feeling unloved and uncared for by his wife. This resentment covered the feelings of disappointment and hurt. "I'm not getting what I want. I don't feel loved," he thinks almost below consciousness. But at the very bottom layer is the fear that "My needs won't be met."

Our first developmental task is to gain a sense of trust as an infant that here in this world we will get our needs met and that we will survive. This husband's basic sense of trust is being shaken with his wife's not preparing meals for him. This is such a primitive feeling that he, as a grown man, will not allow himself to face this fear so he covers it with feeling after feeling for protection. How much more beneficial for the marriage if he could recognize his feelings and share them with his wife. Her assurance may be all he needs, or a compromise where she prepared meals and he helped with the children might be made to alleviate the basic fear. Otherwise they will have many quarrels about other issues instead of the real issue so that resolution is impossible.

People feel many layers of feelings all the time all at once, and these feelings always are changing. This feeling state is a dynamic process that changes continually from moment to moment unless blocked.

It is extremely important to realize that feelings

are not rational. Thoughts are rational but feelings are irrational. Irrational is not to be equated with "bad." Our fast-paced technological society has placed so much emphasis on the rational thinking function within human beings that the equally valuable irrational intuitive feeling function has been neglected and devalued. However, scientists are finding now that both are necessary for optimal functioning, and one without the other is out of balance and less effective.

These two functions are performed by separate hemispheres of the brain. The left hemisphere is the logical thinking analytical portion and the right is the intuitive feeling portion. Today the feeling function a person has is receiving more respect than in the past, as is the realization that the integration of this dual function is needed for complete awareness and subsequent satisfactory growth.

So allow yourself to feel what you feel and allow yourself to be totally aware of these feelings. Recall that feelings are energy and if they are experienced, the energy flows on through the body. Often, however, people keep reciting a litany in their minds about "How awful it is and I just can't stand it," and thereby continue recreating those feelings long after the true feelings are gone. Some people hold on to feelings for years.

One woman, thirty years after the fact, still

remembers in detail and cries broken-heartedly because her husband did not buy her a card on her birthday the first year that they were married but he did for his mother that same year. She tells and retells herself, "His mother must mean more to him than I do and I must not really be very important to him and I always knew that I wasn't worth much anyway." This kind of thinking produces the pain she experiences.

These are not true feelings arising from the person's experience of the moment that provides information about the situation. Whenever feelings last over a few minutes, the person is into a mind game creating and recreating the feelings over and over. Usually this is done to perpetuate a familiar bad feeling, like a self-pity game, or to manipulate their mate with feelings. True feelings are recorded and can then pass away.

Sulking, temper tantrums, self-pity displays, hysteria, crying fits are all illustrations of such manipulation, often felt by the spouse as emotional blackmail. The blackmailer implies, "You **made** me feel this way so you must **make** me feel good again." An impossible situation. People are unaware that they chose to feel that certain feeling and they are completely unaware of their ability to choose a more satisfactory way to feel.

Thus the power over one's feeling state has been

projected out to another, has been disowned entirely, and then the manipulative power struggle begins -- doomed to failure from the beginning because the entire underlying premise is false. No one else **makes** a person feel anything at all. Each person produces his or her own feelings within the body. Other people do, however, have an impact on us. We are affected by the actions of another, but how we feel about that impact is our choice. Hard to believe but true.

People need to listen to their feelings for the information there as opposed to using feelings to manipulate others. This model for working with your feelings is extremely helpful:

1. Be aware of your feelings
2. Experience them in your body
3. Acknowledge them to yourself (Say to yourself, "I am feeling ...")
4. Then the energy will be discharged and will flow on
5. This allows the actual perception of the situation to alter
6. Then decide what you need to do about the situation, if anything. (Sometimes all you need is to feel what you feel and then decide to do nothing).

This model is adapted from one in **Disowned Self** by Nathaniel Branden.

Once a person has listened to the feelings within, then comes the task of communicating those feelings to their spouse so as to insure the growth of their relationship. Otherwise the partner does not know who the spouse is today -- which is very different than yesterday, last year, or the day they married. No one stays the same. Continued communication and negotiation are necessary and valuable for a successful marriage relationship.

If each partner would keep a journal of feelings, writing down what is felt without evaluation, just letting the feelings come as they may, much objective information would be recorded about needs, met and unmet, and the state of the relationship. To do this both parties require the assurance that their journal is private to be able to write freely all their feelings uncensored. Afterwards a synthesis and synopsis of the total picture can be shared with each other and necessary changes to improve the relationship can be possible now.

Sometimes people have shut off feelings to such an extent that they do not know what feeling they are experiencing. People are feeling many feelings every moment of the day, usually several at once. However, there is one feeling in the foreground as others move to the background or on out of the body.

Often conflicting feelings are held simultaneously.

This can make a person feel very crazy but it is normal. For example, a wife may feel afraid because her husband wants to stop with the boys for a beer but she also may feel glad that he trusts her enough to level with her about it, plus feel happy to have a little time alone. Just to know that having conflicting feelings is common, helps a person to accept and understand the conflict experienced.

When feelings are hidden, an excellent and effective exercise is to complete the sentence, "Right now I'm feeling ..." Repeat this several times. Different feelings will surface each time because feelings are always changing. We are always in the process of letting the feeling energy flow out of the body unless the energy is blocked. Always start each sentence with "Right now" because these words will keep your awareness in the present moment and focus on what you are feeling now as opposed to five minutes ago, or last night.

It requires more courage to be aware of the feelings you are feeling at the moment you feel them than to recognize them later. When doing this exercise you might say to yourself, "Right now I'm feeling ridiculous saying this. Right now I'm feeling upset with John. Right now I'm feeling angry because he's so withdrawn. Right now I'm afraid he'll leave me. Right now ..." This process brings to light all the feelings involved, then this information can be noted and action can be taken, if necessary.

If you still have difficulty becoming aware of your feelings, begin with bodily sensations such as, "Right now I'm feeling butterflies in my stomach. Right now I'm feeling a tightness in my throat. Right now I'm feeling like I could easily cry. Right now I'm feeling upset and angry. Right now I'm feeling afraid because John won't talk to me. Right now I'm feeling afraid he's going to leave me." Note that physical feelings will lead to psychological feelings. Our being is communicating to us at all times, in all ways, if we will just be aware enough to listen to the message.

Another very important benefit derived from allowing the energy of feeling to flow is that the tendency to hold the energy in the body is counteracted in this way. In the illustration above, it is evident how the feeling energy was lodged in the stomach and throat. This can become even more serious when the energy is involved in such physical problems as migraine headaches, colitis, high blood pressure, ulcers and more. Current research indicates resentment, held in, is correlated with cancer. So not only emotional health but physical health is dependent on the free flow of the feeling energy. Therefore, allow yourself to feel what you feel. Then you are in a position to choose how you act upon it.

Many people feel controlled or taken over by their feelings. They say, "I just couldn't help it." It seems as if something outside themselves was "possessing" them and making them feel and react in that way. They are completely out of touch with the fact that they themselves are producing that particular feeling. They are out of touch with the power to change it also, or to make themselves feel better.

A person at any moment in time can change his or her feelings by changing the thought process. All feelings flow from thoughts. The thoughts come first. Most people are unaware of the myraid of thoughts **always** flowing in their mind, an internal dialogue is always going on inside. These thoughts are the cause of the feelings experienced. The thoughts are a reaction to what is happening in your outer world or a reaction to the inner picture going on inside of you, which is determined by your philosophy of life.

The process goes something like this: "I can't stand it! He never does it right. He always lets me down. My Daddy never did and if he loved me, he'd do it right. I can't ever depend on him. What will I do?" The feelings will be resentment, hurt, anger and confusion. Or it might be, "I'm so happy. It's so great the way things are with him, just like with Daddy. He always helps me. I know he loves me and I feel so happy and I can't wait until I see him." The resulting feelings in this instance may be happiness, joy, excitement and anticipation.

Roberto Assagioli in **The Act of Will** writes that people become so identified with their feelings, mind, or body that they forget that these are only tools for them to use. The person is more than these tools, more than just a body, more than just a mind, more than just feelings. Assagioli suggests the use of an exercise similar to this:

(Say this several times to yourself)

"I have a **body** but I am not my body. It is an instrument for me to use but it is not me. I have **feelings** but I am not my feelings. They are energy flowing through me bringing me information but they are not me. I have a **mind** but I am not my mind. My mind is a tool of expression but it is not me. I am more than my mind. I am me, a center of pure self-conciousness."

In summary of this chapter on feelings a person might say, "I realize that feelings are important and awareness of them provides information for me about my life situation. They are energy flowing through my body produced by my thoughts. I allow them to flow so they don't get repressed or locked in my physical body, making me ill. I don't use feelings to manipulate others or allow others to manipulate or emotionally blackmail me. I am aware of how I'm feeling at this moment and I communicate this to my spouse so that I will know who I am and that she also will know who I am. My feelings are a tool for me to use. I value them and use them constructively. I always allow myself to feel what I feel."

IV
HAPPINESS BUBBLE, STAGE 1

Identifying the stage

The presentation of the entire model in chapter two was to help you envision the overall process involved in a marriage relationship, specifically in your relationship. Possibly you found yourself in one of the stages in the model and said, "These authors understand me and my marriage. They see my fears."

On the other hand you may have difficulty viewing yourself and your situation clearly and objectively. You may feel, "If I face this, then I'm obligated to do something about it." No obligation is intended. If people try to do something about a situation before they are ready, their mind, in its magic way, will sabotage the efforts anyway.

Therefore, do not put pressure on yourself to make changes until you are ready. You can use the information in this chapter and in the following chapters to learn more about your marriage relationship, the underlying dynamics involved and where you are in the process. Then if you feel ready, utilize the techniques at the end of the chapter to produce change. If you are feeling comfortable where you are in your relationship, stay there. Your feelings of discomfort will tell you when it is time for change.

Found in this Happiness Bubble stage are beginnings of a relationship where dreaming and fantasy are dominant over reality. Most people grow up with the fairy tale idea that they will meet the perfect person, get married, and live happily ever after. Here in this stage of marriage it seems so. Couples feel delighted with one another. She says to herself, "He's just what I've always wanted. I'm happy just being around him." He looks at her and feels so fortunate and fulfilled to have someone who is so beautiful and exciting to be around. They feel happy, fulfilled and very much in love. This is the dynamic process that enables the establishment of the bonding in relationships and the desire to be married.

This stage goes hand in hand with denial, seeing only what one wants to see, denying all that does not fit into the fantasy. The non-verbal contract for the couple is to make believe that "You're perfect and I'm perfect and we'll strive to keep each other happy forever." Gilbert and Sullivan so aptly depicts this in the following song:

WHEN A MERRY MAIDEN MARRIES

When a merry maiden marries,
Sorrow goes and pleasures tarries;
Every sound becomes a song,
All is right, and nothing's wrong!
From today and ever after let our tears be tears of laughter,
Every sigh that finds a vent be a sigh of sweet content!

When you marry, merry maiden,
Then the air with love is laden;
Every flower is a rose, every goose becomes a swan,
Every kind of trouble goes where the last year's snows have gone!
Sunlight takes the place of shade when you marry, merry maid!
Every sound becomes a song, all is right and nothing's wrong!

(from ***The Gondoliers*** *by Gilbert and Sullivan)*

This Happiness Bubble can be maintained as long as the spouses can recognize each other's expectations and fantasies and meet them. Sometimes this stage lasts only until the honeymoon is over and sometimes it lasts for years. It depends on how much energy the couple is willing to invest in maintaining the illusion that all is well. "He's my Prince Charming and I'm his Princess." As long as the payoff is worth more than the hassle, this can continue. The fear is allayed and it "feels" as if the relationship is secure. One has asked to be cared for by another person who is the answer to his or her dreams. They have achieved this and intend to maintain it. "Only let me hear what I want to hear" is the unspoken demand.

Behavior of the denial stage looks like this: Betsy who is pretty and is smart in the ways of making a man happy, comes home from the office and starts dinner, pours a glass of wine, or mixes a drink, or refreshes her makeup waiting for the return of her hard-working man. Enter Bill. He comes in, takes his drink, exchanges slight notes on the day, and retires behind his paper or the mail. The couple has dinner, watches TV for the evening, maybe discusses the purchase of a new couch, and later makes love and awakens to start over once again. In itself the above scene is tranquil. However, underneath is the disappointment and hurt of having the expectations of closeness, or the opportunity to discuss and possibly resolve a real hurt, be unavailable or absent.

There is a refusal to face anything that is less than perfect and the problems are swept from awareness. The key phrases at this stage are, "I can be happy with you. You are going to do it for me. **You** make me happy. It's all okay just as it is." This is the language of fantasy. Tremendous energy is expended keeping the spouse on the pedestal. This seems necessary because, at this point in the development of the marital relationship, the spouse is seen as a god or savior who makes the partner happy and complete. A spouse may say, "With you I can be a complete person, I feel whole and safe and secure."

The denial found here is not totally bad, it is a natural part of the development of a relationship and is a prerequisite to other stages. Denial is an everday experience that your mind uses to filter out many of the thoughts and feelings so that your mind will not get cluttered with unnecessary thoughts. Denial is needed to retain perspective on life and to insure that we will not spend all our time remembering only the bad things that have happened to us in the past. The mind, in its miraculous fashion, denies past hurts to prepare us and make us receptive to new relationships. Our goal is to understand what denial is so that we can choose to let it operate, or stop it when it is non-functional. It is not necessary or healthy to get angry with yourself for denying. Just be aware of what you are doing and then choose whether or not you want to continue.

The problem lies in becoming entrapped at this

point and never progressing on to the natural developmental levels that are a part of a satisfying marital relationship. This is analogous to the natural growth and developmental stages in a child. To be in the negative two-year-old stage is necessary for balanced growth in later stages, but it becomes a block when the child is stuck there and cannot flow on with the natural, sequential process of development.

Relationships need fantasy. In the beginning couples do not entirely know one another, and fantasy or imagining what the spouse is like is necessary to be able to achieve the beginning process in relating to another person. Marriages also need a vision of what will be ... a dream of tomorrow and "How we will be together," which produces the desire to stay together and make a commitment.

When people believe this fantasy is reality, or if they attempt to fit the spouse or themselves into that fantasy, distorting their own true nature, then the results are disasterous. This is an awareness that marriage partners need for their own personal growth and for the marriage relationship to progress satisfactorily on to future stages. Otherwise the relationship becomes rigidly locked in, preventing growth. The paradox applicable here is to let go and let the spouse and the relationship be what they are, and allow the natural process to flow. This is a good way to keep the marriage alive. Anything held on to rigidly will die. Letting go is the best way to have the relationship.

Awareness of the actual reality of the relationship, of the spouse, and of oneself, is important so that choice in these areas can be maintained. Couples need to be the master who determines where the relationship moves so that they can guide it into directions where they each feel satisfied and fulfilled. When we are not aware of what actually is happening, then we are victims of the force of an unconscious process, which is particularly potent because we have no conscious choice about the situation. Ideally we want to be **consciously** choosing what our life is to be.

When couples are so rigidly holding on to the dream of what the marriage is to be, they are future oriented, living in what is to be, and missing the here-and-now everyday aspects of their relationship as it really is. They have a screen of expectations through which they must filter today's experiences of the spouse and of the relationship. This limits drastically. Much of the pleasure that is outside of the fantasy is missed. Many of the problems are simply not faced and are left to grow. Sometimes they grow so large they kill the relationship. It is so much more beneficial to be aware of all that the marriage and spouse actually are in the here-and-now, to live in the present as opposed to the future because the present-day experience is where life truly is -- not in mind trips about the future.

We have discussed denial and fantasy as aspects that characterize this Happiness Bubble stage. Dependency also is found here. When we deny parts of ourselves and do not see ourselves as a whole person, we need someone else to make us feel whole and complete again. How often a marriage partner feels fulfilled when he or she is with the spouse, yet cannot feel happy alone. This is dependence on another person to make you feel complete, safe and secure.

We are more satisfied when we realize that we are whole alone, that we have all the power and potential we need, that our happiness comes from within -- not from the spouse.

However, in this Happiness Bubble phase we do not realize this clearly and are dependent on the spouse for security and happiness in order to feel fulfilled. When we rely on the spouse like this, we are very concerned about what they do, how they look, what they say, how they think, every aspect of them. If your wife is part of you, then you have to keep her in line, control her and make her fit into the fantasy so that your dreams can be fulfilled and your self-image kept intact.

When the realization begins to dawn on one

person that the spouse may not be living up to the fantasy, fear creeps in. At this point manipulation is begun and pressure in covert ways is put on the spouse to be like he or she is supposed to be in the other's mind. Maintenance of the fantasy is top priority now.

For example, a young couple went out with friends and the young man began to have a few drinks. The young woman, feeling frightened because her father was an alcoholic, began to manipulate the situation so that her fear would go away and she could feel comfortable again. She knew she could not tolerate a relationship with him if he drank heavily so she began to manipulate him by saying, "I'm so glad you don't drink a lot like my father or other men." Then he thinks to himself, "She won't want to stay with me if I drink and I can't live without her, so I'll have to stop what I enjoy to be with her." He carefully hides from himself his anger at this limitation. She thinks, "I can't tell him how afraid his or anyone's drinking makes me; I can't ask for what I want or need so I'll just hint. And if he loves me, he won't drink."

Little comments like these, when the cryptic messages underneath are understood, can hold a relationship at the same level for many years, maintaining the fantasy that he does not like to drink when, in fact, he might enjoy a few. This nondrinking behavior was what the man had to do to fill the expectation of this young woman, allaying her fears carried into the relationship from her childhood. How much more productive it would have been if she could have been honest about her fears and asked for what she needed from him, then he would have had an opportunity to make a free choice. "When you drink I feel afraid and I need reassurance that you won't be like my father." That process would strengthen a relationship because it is free of manipulation and of repression of the fear and anger.

When we need a partner to be a certain way for us, and we are dependent on this partner to meet our needs, we are caught in a parent-child type relationship. Here one partner is thought to have more power than the other, just as a parent has more power than a child. The child needs to be taken care of, decisions need to be made for the child. A child usually has to resort to manipulation to get needs met by the parents through such methods as self-pity, withdrawing, anger, temper tantrums, fearful behavior, illness, or being a people-pleaser. As a dependent adult, we revert back to these behaviors to try and get our needs met by our spouse.

It is interesting to observe that when one member of a pair is dependent, so is the other. A self-reliant person does not allow someone to lean on him or her. The parent-child relating will switch, having one partner be the decision-making parent in one area -- such as in money matters -- and the other assuming the parent role in another area -- such as in school activities with the kids, where one tells the other how they should be acting. The word "should" is a clue that lets you know when you are in the parent role. Parents always know the best way things "should" be done.

The goal is to be two self-reliant, whole people living together in a loving, sharing relationship where each person ends up enhanced, being more together than alone.

Each stage has characteristic rituals. A ritual of this first stage might be that every birthday, occasion, anniversary must be remembered or love is lost. Another might be to have sex every night after the news. There are positive aspects to rituals but the danger is going along with the ritual just because it has been established. Your needs have changed but the ritual is still acted out in the same old way, unquestioned.

The subject of looks is affected by the fantasy of stage one. "I must take care of my body so that my husband and people will think I'm good looking, slim and attractive. I must be attractive, and my husband should not see me in curlers or with my face all messed up crying, or he won't love me." Energy is spent on the maintenance of the facade. "You'll need never go to anyone else because I'll be so beautiful and I'll spend my energy selling you on that point." Underneath is the fear, "You will hurt me by rejecting me and find someone else more attractive, thereby defining me as inadequate. I am dependent for my sense of worth on what you think of me, so I have to be careful how I look."

In the Happiness Bubble stage described here, the power struggle almost always is manipulative and covert -- hidden and not out in the open like the normal definition of fighting. As the couple passes into the next stage, the power struggle and the control mechanisms become overt and obvious. In this first stage, however, energy is spent denying that any problems exist or that there is any defect in the once promised love.

Theoretical perspectives

The life of a marriage has a process, a step-by-step progression through developmental stages. It is often helpful to view a stage of human development through the lens of several known therorists.

Erik Erikson, for example, states in **Childhood and Society** that the growing human child progresses through eight stages of psycho-social development on his way to becoming a socially funtional adult. Erikson bases his stages on those previously designated by Freud. The first Freudian stage of human development is the meeting of oral (mouth) needs. The infant develops trust dependent on whether or not his need to be fed is met. Maybe this is why many of our first contacts as adults are for meals, to meet our oral body needs.

In the infant relationship, the first stage for Erikson can be seen as devoted to resolving the basic attitude of "trust vs mistrust." He defines trust as "an essential trustfulness of others as well as a fundamental sense of one's own trustworthiness."

In a budding relationship, the trust issues revolve around such questions as: "Can I trust my partner to arrive on time? Can I trust my spouse to come right home to dinner?" Trust is developed by having these questions answered satisfactorily, time and time again.

We use, as a criteria for choosing a partner, whether or not we can trust the person to come through for us, and whether or not we can trust ourselves to do the same for our partner such that he or she will be motivated to stay. "Can I trust him to come home even when I'm bitchy? Can I trust her to remain faithful even when I must travel?" Without asking the questions of trust, we find no anchor upon which to fasten ourselves together.

If the answers we discover have even the slightest possibility of shattering the newly-budding dream romance, we use what Freud calls a "defense mechanism." This is an unconscious thought process designed to " ... neutralize the potentially upsetting impact of threatening events or ideas by distorting reality in small but significant ways." The defense mechanism present in stage 1 of marriage is denial.

Denial is discussed as the first attitude toward grieving over something or someone treasured that was lost. Elizabeth Kubhler-Ross, whose work with terminally ill cancer patients is classic, speaks about grief, the grief of the dying and the grief of the loved one. She discussed five stages of resolving grief, the grief of death, or generalized, the grief over great change affecting our lives.

Our first tendency, when we find ourselves in unknown waters instead of those situations with which we are familiar, is to deny as many fearful aspects as possible. For example, when one woman found herself swept into the middle of a new relationship, she suddenly asked, "Do I trust this fellow to keep the terrific promises he's made? Of course, he wouldn't promise if he hadn't meant to keep them." When we say "of course," that's where we permit the fear to pass unattended, and that's denial.

It is a common belief today that defense mechanisms are bad, neurotic and weak. On the contrary, however, we use a defense mechanism when we are afraid and in need of defense. Feeling afraid is human, in fact, a survival trait built in for our safety. So when our survival or situation is threatened, we defend, in an attempt to maintain the status quo. The defense mechanism shields us from facing ideas before we are ready so we will not feel overwhelmed.

William Schutz in his **Interpersonal Underworld** states that people cycle through meeting their needs for inclusion, control and affection. The first of these needs is inclusion, how we include the new partner in our life. "How much attention do I want to give this person and how much attention do I want demonstrated to me? How many times can I go out with the boys without including you? How often will we include each other in evening meals? How much do you want to be included in my work?"

Thus, while we are resolving the basic issue of how much we trust the new person through the medium of how much time we spend together, we use the defense mechanism of denial whenever we hit a snag or come up with some need we have unmet in the relationship.

Abraham Maslow says human needs have an order of being met. The needs for physiological tending, like eating, breathing, eliminating, cleaning are the most important to meet first. Who could concentrate on a problem if they are really hungry, or thirsty, or cold? So, says Maslow, before we can even think about meeting other needs, we must see to these bodily-function needs first.

In the beginning of a relationship, the needs that are tended are our first order of needs, those to be included, trusted, nurtured. These needs are the functioning needs like cooking meals, doing the wash, shopping, car repair which comprise our first decisions and build trust together. We raise a relationship as we raise a child, from infancy through the stages of development to mature and comfortable functioning.

Sex

This is one of the most intriguing, exciting and powerful areas in a male-female relationship. Yet it is one of the most confusing and obscure. Very few couples have the rapport to communicate verbally about sex, especially the specifics about "What turns me on and what turns you on." This type discussion probably is the most revealing, threatening and vulnerable that a couple can have.

Our whole society has had difficulty dealing with sex and all its ramifications, and not until recently has sex been more openly discussed. Even with this new openness, it is only about sex in general, the personal sexual feelings, preferences and behavior rarely are shared.

As a result, couples get into fantasies of how sex should be in their bedroom. Unspoken rules about how the couple is to be together sexually are established quickly and wordlessly. There are rules specifying whether or not each person has permission to seduce or be seduced. One partner possibly can violate the other's sexual expectations by being, in the bedroom, a different person than in the living room. Oftimes one person does not keep his or her body as clean as the partner would need to feel turned on, creating a problem area. If the couple is using denial, still attempting to maintain the fantasy that they have married the perfect mate, those feelings are repressed to do damage later. Also, the problem does not get corrected, allowing resentment and estrangement to grow.

Many couples decide, wordlessly, that some material is just too risky to discuss, and sex usually is the first in this category. They have not built enough trust with each other to feel free to discuss this area. One couple had a marriage that was two years old before the husband felt comfortable enough to confess that he was a virgin at the time of their marriage. With another couple a crisis point came in their marriage when she came close to death. The seriousness of what happened at that time allowed her to finally realize that her husband was trustworthy enough to discuss sexual issues with, but unfortunately it took a crisis to do so.

The major issue of trust has to be resolved before couples can deal effectively with the dynamically-loaded area of sex. Trust is difficult to build when denial is ever present.

Social situation

Also, in the first stage of marriage couples have to resolve how they are going to present themselves as a pair to the world. Usually this area is never discussed either. Each person has an idea inside about how married couples should be at parties, with friends, with relatives. Since they are into this picture of how they should act, and denying all that does not fit into that picture, many power struggles, usually covert, ensue. Each partner is fighting for their picture to be fulfilled. she may say "I like you so much better when you wear your blue suit to Mother's. You look so handsome." Inside she is still trying to get her Mother's approval much as she did in the first grade when she brought new friends home from school.

At this point couples cannot allow their spouse to be real. The investment is too high. "My identity is tied up in you so in order for me to feel safe in the world, you have to be how I picture you," is the unconscious message inside. There is a basic lack of trust that if the partner is just who he or she is, that all will be alright.

It is important to realize that all aspects of a couple's relationship will be changed by the way they decide to change behavior and feelings. As a person changes, he or she will become a new person with which to experience sex just as he or she will become a new person with whom to eat breakfast.

New experiences stimulate growth in people and relationships and this encourages people to continue to change. Life is movement, movement requires change; therefore, to grow in life, change is necessary. Wherever you are in the growth of your marriage or of yourself, it is okay.

All stages and changes, or the lack of change, is acceptable. Wherever you are is simply wherever you are. Acceptance is seeing a situation as it is. Acceptance is not synonymous with approval. Many people feel reluctant to be accepting because they think that is the same as giving their approval to whatever is happening. All that is necessary is to realize that you are here now, this is where you are supposed to be, and then if you choose you can move on. Your marriage will not be defined as "good" only if you end up in stage five. All stages are necessary and attainable.

An oak tree is perfectly alright as an acorn, as a young sapling with new tender growth, as a larger sturdy tree, or when it is an ancient, gnarled, huge tree. Each stage is part of the growth process and is natural. So it is with the marriage growth process.

Children and household duties

When a couple is in the Happiness Bubble stage and the maintenance of the fantasy is top priority, children are affected by this. With the parents denying their true feelings in order to keep the dream alive, the children learn quickly that in this family anger or true feelings are not expressed and family members work together to maintain the illusion that all is well.

Some children are caught in this process, profoundly limiting their growth and the expression of their true feelings and true self. Other children become the "bad child," the one family member who acts out all the negative feelings for the other members who are trapped in the illusion of total happiness and goodness. Both of these positions generally are detrimental for the normal development of the child. Some children insulate themselves and grow anyway.

There are tremendous expectations placed on the children to live up to the fantsy of perfection. After all, princes and princesses cannot have just ordinary, dirty, active children. Their children must be wonderful all the time. A child soon learns that he or she is not alright as is. This undermines their developing sense of self-esteem. These children grow up with a dissatisfaction about themselves, striving always to perfect themselves or maybe failing because of a poor self-image.

This is an over-simplification of an infinitely complex subject. Children are affected by a myriad of factors including their own internal conclusions. We intend only to touch on the issue for some awareness of the affect on children.

Sometimes there is a transference of the dependency found in this stage of marriage from the spouse to the child. Many women who feel no value alone and need a man to make them feel whole and complete incorporate the children and place pressure on the children to be perfect in order to be not only a good wife but now a good mother.

Husbands, who are a top-sargent type, need others to control. They are dependent on them and need to tell them what to do and how to be in order for all to go as he thinks it should. Sometimes this is accomplished with loving pressure, ("I'm only doing this for your own good."), or with outward force, ("Do as I say, I'm your father.").

Dependency can be a trap for the woman who feels she is not free to grow and express herself in this world as she actually is. She believes she has to play a part of wife and mother at the expense of her real self. This is a two-way street because this dependency also traps the husband and children, since none of them are free to grow as they really are. All of them must live up to complex expectations that each one is placing on the others.

Struggles over the roles to be filled require vast amounts of energy during this stage. A wife tells her husband, "I'm so glad you intend to keep the yard nice like my Dad did, Honey," covertly putting pressure on him to fulfill the role the way she needs in order to have her dream world intact.

He may think, "I hate yard work, but if I do this she'll have to cook me a good dinner like my Mom always did and the kids will help pull weeds rather than going swimming. Later we can sit out front and enjoy the yard and the neighbors will approve and think our yard looks great."

Everyone comes into marriage with an idea in mind of who is to do what. The role expectations have been learned from their families of origin. Most couples are not even aware of these biases. They usually feel that this is just the way it is to be. They do not sit down and negotiate who is to do what, who likes to do which tasks, what actually needs to be done, especially when in stage one because that might burst the Hapiness Bubble and, at all costs, that must be preserved. How much covered-up pain could be avoided if an open discussion of feelings about children and household duties could be held.

The couple could help each other with the household duties and the task of parenting if only the denial and fantasy were not in the way. The parents and children would experience less tension because when issues are discussed and resolved, much of the stress will be released instead of hidden to do damage.

There are many ways to nurture and in this overweight nation we link food and love together far too often. Husbands who are trying to watch weight are not helped by a wife who insists that to show you love her, you must clean your plate. Children who are trying to test the reality of the world will say, "I don't want to eat. I'm not hungry." A food-nurturer inhibits this natural testing. The mother is saying in effect, "Listen, don't you know that my worth and value as a person and a good mother are based on whether or not you eat this now."

Loving and nurturing each other are better not demonstrated with food, as people often erroneously believe. How much better, however, could it be communicated in such ways as touching, eye contact, smiling at each other, listening and really hearing the other person, and, most effective of all, sharing your feelings with them. Telling them you care, you like being with them, you appreciate this and that, and you love them.

Nurturing through communication eliminates the need people have to fill up that scared, lonely, empty feeling inside with food.

Communication

At this Happiness Bubble stage communication is limited to areas considered safe. All the areas needed to be talked about but do not fit into the fantasy are carefully avoided. Disappointments and resentments are pushed out of awareness and silence or false smiles replace them. Therefore communication is not open, free, complete or very effective. The primary goal is to keep the fantasy alive and continue the illusion that "I am perfect, you are perfect, and together we'll be completely happy."

Communication becomes future-oriented. You might find yourself saying, "When this happens ..., I wish that ..., If only we had... " By watching language to spot such evidence that you are looking to the future to relieve the pain of the present, then you can begin to change your phrases. "I am enjoying this now because ..., Right now, I would like to...."

Patterns of how couples communicate will be developed at this phase only along the lines of safe areas. For instance, one woman came from a family where conflict and verbal fighting were seen as bad. Family members never yelled at one another because it was not safe. Her husband came from a family where yelling was their method of healing and resolution. Unless you yelled and then made up, there was never a resolution. Their difference produced an instant communication mixup. They could not resove anything because it could not be discussed since it did not fit into their total happiness fantasy derived from her family of origin.

When a situation such as this exists, it is necessary to put energy into manipulation in an attempt to resolve the dilemma. The power struggle has begun on a covert, undercover level. It will not appear as an open struggle, however, until the couple moves on to the next stage where the anger felt makes the parties enemies.

A common conversation in this Happiness Bubble phase might go like this: "What do you want to do tonight, Honey?" "Oh, I don't know. What do you want to do?" "Well, we could go to a movie if you want to." "That would be okay, what do you want to see." "I don't know, what do you want to see?" These two partners are so fearful of rocking the boat that they can hardly decide anything. Both are blocked off from being aware of their wants or needs. Any other method of communication feels too risky to employ at this time.

Another illustration might sound like this: "Let's go to the movies and see the spooky horror show, and then go see John and Betty." "Okay, darling," she replies, feeling downhearted but smiling delightedly. She hates horror pictures and is uncomfortable around John and Betty, but never says so because she imagines he'd be angry and that feels intolerable.

One or both parties are very sensitive and tuned into the partner, trying to read the messages being sent out verbally and non-verbally. The eyes are watched to read what the partner is feeling, all body movements are noted and a slight turn of the head can be interpreted as things are not all right so straighten up and make everything okay.

The goal in all this is to make the relationship be a certain way in order to feel safe and secure. Quite a tall order when open communication is too frightening and they are left to guess about what the partner is feeling. Assumptions cause tremendous problems because people make wrong assumptions so often. Yet when these cannot be checked out with the partner, then a false assumption is reacted to as if it were truth.

For example, Mary and Dick had been at her Mother's for dinner. Dick was quieter than usual. Every time Mary's Mother spoke, Dick got a pained expression on his face. Mary felt scared inside. She tried to draw them together and tried to manipulate her Mother into saying Dick was great so that Dick would feel more relaxed. Mary needed them to be friends because she was dependent on both of them. She'd say to her Mother, "Tell Dick what you said to me last week about how you liked the way he'd fixed the garage shelves," and other such statements. The evening became no better.

Mary was more and more afraid. Later in bed she was too tied in knots to enjoy sex and both turned over unhappy and silent. If Mary and Dick could have been communicating openly, she could have checked out her assumption with him and found that it was his deceased Mother's birth date and the pain of his past loss was surfacing once again and was increased by being with Mary's Mother. Mary could not ask what was wrong and Dick could not share his feelings because grown men don't cry, of course. His pain was so great he was afraid to face it himself, much less discuss it, even with Mary.

Tremendous resentment, hostility and unresolved issues are being repressed during this stage, stored up to injure each person emotionally and often physically, and to injure the relationship eventually. Yet the outward picture is sweetness and light. Both the powerful negative feelings and the enjoyable positive feelings always live side by side in the relationship in this, as in all, stages. Marriage when most productive allows not only the "good" but also the "bad" areas to be recognized, talked about and experienced. Yet this is not part of the Happiness Bubble.

Work and play

The relationship can be loads of fun in this stage. The newness is exciting. Each partner is so willing to be with the beloved that it is just fun being together. Thoughts of how to please each other keep an extraordinary amount of enjoyment and play alive in the relationship at this point. Since conflict is denied, most days are delightful -- at least outwardly.

The work area becomes important because now, "We are working together." The husband may feel keenly the pressure society puts on him to succeed as a breadwinner. He does not have permission, being a prince and all, to talk about or even recognize his fear of failure, his fear of being responsible, his own needs to be supported and cared for himself. He buries these feelings and plunges into the work world. This pressure will often make him very successful on the job. Employees know this and feel a married man is a more stable employee than a single man. Society has dictated to him that he has something to work for now. Seeming success but what of the fear and resentment buried, to do damage later. Many a longtime married man will say, "All I am is a paycheck to you, you don't care about me."

Feelings denied are like sweeping trash under the rug. It will eventually begin to foul up the relationship.

Self-concept

Your idea of yourself that you formed as a child was derived from others around you, and you came to rely on your own opinion of yourself more as you matured. What Mama and Daddy said about you and how they treated you was particularly influential. This concept expanded in a complex way as time passed and you grew up. But now you are in the Happiness Bubble and, once again, your self-concept is tied to someone outside yourself. How the spouse treats you, how he or she looks, what this person says or does, all define who you are.

Many a husband will tell his wife how to dress, what to say at parties, how much to drink, and more. He must guard carefully what she does for she must be his princess because his self-concept depends on it. She must be perfect in order for him to feel safe.

The spouse is an extension of oneself. A clear idea of oneself from within is difficult when in this stage. Not until the Self-Discovery stage is achieved can this be accomplished.

Techniques and tools

We plan to present information and exercises you

can utilize at each stage under this heading in each chapter about the five stages of marriage.

How to find the feelings and fears

Most problems in a relationship have basic underlying fears and a myriad of feelings entangled into a complex web of different issues. A helpful exercise for discovering your feelings is to, first, tune into your physical body. It is always communicating to you about your feelings. Check out for areas of tension. See if you are "up tight." If so, ask yourself, "What is happening to me?" ... and listen as you answer that question in your head. All the information we need to make ourselves happy is inside already.

You may try talking with that "up tight" part of your body. For instance, "I'm Jane's stomach. I'm 'up tight' and in knots. And I'm feeling sick and tired of all this charade of putting on a smile and saying it's alright when it isn't." A troubled relationship is manifested here as a troubled stomach.

Also, you can write down your feelings. Allow yourself, for a minute or two, to write whatever comes to you. Valuable information is gained about feelings, fears and your relationship this way. You can tear it up immediately if need be, but at least the knowledge is yours and that is the job of feelings -- to bring you information.

At this point you can choose freely to do something to improve the situation or choose to leave it as is. The pain may be easier to deal with than the imagined confrontation at this point. But at least you are **choosing.**

How to change your attitude

If you discover that most of the difficulty is due primarily to your attitude, you have the power to change it. You created your attitude and you and only you can change it.

Write down all the negative beliefs you have in a certain area. Decide how you want to feel, what attitude would be more productive. Then write the new attitude beside the old negative belief. Later cross out the negative ones as a symbol to your subconcious mind that you are eliminating them.

Example:

Old Beliefs
I'm always unhappy
Things never turn out right.
No one ever loves me.
I can't make it on my own.

New Attitudes
I am happy alot of the time.
Life is going well.
I am loved.
I can make it.

Then follow these steps:

1. Begin each morning with this process when you **first** wake up and are still in bed.
   a) **Think** about the new attitude and what you want.
   b) **See** pictures of it in your mind in detail.
   c) **Say** the new attitudes you wrote down ten times.

2. Do this again when you go to bed and are **relaxed.** The subconscious mind which affects our life experiences is best activated or programmed with new information when you are relaxed. If you are interested in learning more about this process, read **Psychocybernetics** by Maxwell Maltz.

3. Throughout the day think of what you want. Put up reminder notes about how you want it. Eliminate any thinking about what you do not want. Think, see and feel the situation as you want it. Do this as often as you desire. The more you think of it, the sooner the desired outcome. The more intense energy we put into something, whether positive or negative, the more effective the results. Any time and every time you think of the negative side of the situation, go through the process again.

This is not anything new and different. You are doing it all day, every day anyway. It is our natural process but we are misusing it. We produce what we put our energy into. What we fear, love, want or believe is of extreme importance because we will get it for sure. It is the law of the universe.

Give it a try! What do you have to lose? Maybe the bad feelings, maybe being the victim?

The attitude a person has affects the way life unfolds. Whatever a person puts mental energy into is manifested in life in some way. If you believe long enough that life is miserable, it will be. So control your thinking and stop thinking about lack and negativity.

In addition, you can ask yourself,

"What is it I fear will happen if I **don't** change?"

"What is it I fear will happen if I **do** change?"

Then list the fears that you become aware of as you ask these questions. These are resistances to allowing your life to be as you want it to be.

Next, release each fear. Let them go. Talk with yourself and explain why each one is unfounded. Every time fear arises in your mind, say to yourself: "I let this fear go and I allow myself to ____________."

A healthy attitude is essential. Everything in your life is affected by your attitude, this includes your behavior.

How to change your behavior

The total person includes the body, mind, feelings

and spirit. When we desire change in our lives, we may choose any one of these levels to focus on for a change. When we do, the other areas will experience a corresponding change because we are an integrated whole being and all aspects affect one another. So to produce a happier state of mind, you can change your behavior.

You have seen people who walk with a spring in their step, their chin thrust forward ... obviously people on the move. You, too, can concentrate on walking this way. This may sound like play-acting but, in reality, the springy step encourages energy to flow in your body and your whole metabolism becomes quickened, and the chin forward frees the windpipe from obstructions and pressure so that oxygen can be taken in easily. This same oxygen gets to the brain and you feel good. You changed your behavior and then your attitude and feelings changed.

Ultimately you need to be certain there is a change in your belief system -- the ideas in your mind -- or you will revert back to the old way easily. Everything always begins as an idea in mind first.

When in stage 1, you may feel like you are in a bubble in the air, wide-eyed, above reality. If you want to be more grounded, imagine yourself standing on the earth, solidly planted here, standing straight and tall, feeling secure and in charge of yourself. An exercise such as this can change how you feel and how you behave.

You may have noticed that your behavior when you are alone is very divergent from when you are in the presence of others because you are so often a representative self playing-like everything is alright. After doing this imagining exercise above, your behavior alone and in public will match more closely because you will be less afraid and more secure in being yourself -- not playing the part of the perfect counterpart to a perfect spouse.

How to deal with staying in a stage by choice

It may be that you have decided that you are in this stage and are happy here. The dream life is wonderful if you have enough energy to maintain it. In fact, maybe it requires less energy to stay in the fantasy stage than it does to move forward. The fantasy can be secure and enveloping, or circumstances can allow you to feel that you cannot afford to be questioning now.

Maybe you have several young children, or see this relationship as a sink-or-swim situation. Then maybe you cannot feel safe enough to change. When there are young children in the home, the mother needs to have the father do some parenting for a while so she can get some of her own needs met, even if it is just to take a hot bath. The fear is that moving on would risk his support when she so desperately needs it.

Personal growth, especially when it requires moving out of a carefully constructed cocoon, takes energy. Change always requires an expenditure of energy. The payoff, however, would be that less energy is being spent on staying in this stage than would be needed for a change.

Another young mother says, "If I had moved to the stage of questioning and being angry, I would have given my children bad vibs and they would have been affected by my angry behavior. As it was, staying in the Happiness Bubble let me nurture my children and relinquish my concern about myself for a time. I could focus my energy and attention on child care and not deal with the underneath part that was waiting to be resolved some time later. I'm glad I waited."

Then there is the woman who said that she decided, subconciously, to remain in this denial stage because the reality would be so painful to face and a decision would be forced. Therefore, she maintained the fantasy at all costs until she was strong enough to deal with the pain that was inherent in facing the reality of her situation. Giving yourself permission to be where you are is a tool. Say to yourself often, "Doing what I'm doing now takes care of me and that's okay."

How to work with an unwilling partner

The first thing you usually do is go through all your repertoire of manipulating techniques to get your partner to want to grow with you, such as, leaving growth books around, asking your partner to think about changing, trying to make your partner ashamed that you are doing all the work. This doesn't help.

Upon finding yourself here in the Happiness Bubble, wanting a change, and realizing that your partner is still heavily basking in the false glory of the fantasy relationship and unwilling, usually out of fear, to look at the reality of it all, you can begin to tell your partner about what you are feeling. This takes courage but it is more productive than the manipulative techniques we usually use.

We are our most vulnerable selves when we share our feelings. We have learned to maintain a safe distance by communicating about things -- cars, children, concepts -- sharing our ideas about them as opposed to our feelings.

You bring change into the relationship when your feelings are shared. Your unwilling spouse may be resistant and afraid. When Mary realized she was playing the part of a happy princess, she decided to level and said to John, "I didn't tell you last week when we went to Bill and Jane's house that I don't enjoy them. I feel like a fake and I wasn't being real with you. I plan to tell you what I'm really feeling in the future, and I'd like you to tell me what you really feel also." Mary is telling (1) what she feels and (2) what she wants -- a good technique.

However, John may retort, "You used to like my friends. What's getting into you anyhow? That's not like you, " attempting to get her to be the compliant, loving wife of the past. John may feel inside, "If she doesn't like my friends, she doesn't like me and she may want to leave and I can't stand that. I can't live without her." He is frightened and tries to get her to be like she used to be in an attempt to keep the Happiness Bubble from bursting.

Mary is illustrating a way to be yourself in a non-manipulative way and is telling her spouse what is going on with her.

Or a spouse could say, "I'm working on some changes that I'm not sure I'm ready to share yet, not because I don't love you but because it's scary. I'll try to let you know what it's all about as soon as I can get confident and comfortable." In effect you are giving a little speech about yourself. Even if you meet with non-concern or ridicule, you know that you have been absolutely honest.

A shorter version says, "I'm really confused right now about myself and it makes me afraid." No more. Just a statement of where you are at the time.

All communication loses any and all effect if it is used in a manipulative way. You might say to your spouse, "I'm really confused right now," and know that the hesitancy in your voice will make him respond with the responsible part of himself that tries to make everything okay and say, "Oh, Honey, are you mad? Did I do something wrong?" His fear is hooked and then he puts out a colossal amount of energy to change your feelings. This is a waste of time and energy.

A more positive use of energy is to do some reflective listening with your unwilling spouse. Reflective listening is where you act as a mirror reflecting back the sense of what the spouse is saying, not adding anything new. For instance, John might say: "This psychology stuff is for the birds so get off my back." Mary could reflect back, "You think I'm pushing you with these ideas I read." He may reply, "Yes, they don't know what I'm feeling anyway." She responds, "You think they don't know or understand your pain?" "Right. A man needs to take care of his family himself." She could reflectively reply, "You feel you need to do it alone?" He might say, "No, I mean **we** need to do it. No one else can tell me what to do to make things better." She replies, "You feel you need to do it yourself and you want our marriage improved." He answers, "Yes, you know we're unhappy."

This reflective listening technique helps move a person out of the emotional fog they are in because it helps them become clear about the situation. Much like when you look in the mirror and see you hair mussed, then you can decide whether or not to comb it. But until you realized it was a mess, you had no desire to do anything about it.

This is an excellent communication tool that helps a person to become aware of the situation. One of the biggest trouble-makers in a marriage relationship is lack of awareness.

When experimenting with new communication and sharing your feelings, be sure to include your positive feelings about how you honestly feel about your partner and his or her behavior. In essence, talk about the aspects you appreciate rather than only the aspects that displease you. This will contribute to a feeling of safety and trust which is an encouraging atmosphere for growth.

All growth would stop if people had to wait for others to be in the exact same psychological space as they are and sometimes you need to move on without your partner. When you feel discomfort strongly enough, you will feel the impetus for change and will be unwilling to wait for your spouse.

Now and then one partner chides the other, pushing for change before he or she is ready. Like a flower beginning to bloom, if someone wants to hasten it up and pulls the petals apart, the flower will be killed in the process. Human beings, like flowers, grow best at their own rate. Therefore, continue your own growth but at the same time give your spouse freedom to be where he or she is. Remember to share and share again your feelings with your mate.

Yes, share your feelings with your partner but do not use them to try to change him or her. That is manipulation and only puts the two of you in a battle for control -- a battle in which both sides end up losers.

Susan would manipulatively say to Fred, "I feel that you should be more considerate with my Mother. You always are so tacky to her. If you loved me, you wouldn't treat her this way." This is manipulation. She is out to get it her way.

On the other hand Jane says to Bill, "I feel unhappy when I'm around the hassels between you and Mom. I want you to consider being easier on her so I can stand to be around the two of you." Jane is leveling, sharing her feelings and asking outright for what she wants. Bill is free to choose how he will be. This is not manipulation. Maybe he will choose to "blow it off" but at least it is manipulation-free.

A word of caution is in order here. Watch the "I feel ..." statements with the word **that** in them. The word **that** is a clue to manipulation. This is a hidden, attacking "You" statement. A more effective way is to say, "I feel..." and immediately follow with a feeling word, such as, unhappy, mad, frustrated, glad, afraid. When feelings are shared, the mate has an opportunity to correct misperceptions -- the beginning steps in problem solving. But when manipulative techniques are employed, all the partner can do is defend or counterattack and all the energy goes into battle rather than resolution.

Be gentle and understanding with yourself, none of us human beings are perfect. We all learned manipulative ways to get our needs met. This is how we survived. This is what we were taught. Don't be ashamed of this. Just realize it helped you to get here. The point is that there is a better way. No one else wants to be manipulated. Everyone needs to be free, so straight, leveling methods are more effective. Don't put a guilt-trip on yourself whenever you find yourself being manipulative, just change to a better way.

How to work with a willing partner

Maybe both of you are willing to share feelings and learn together. How fortunate you are. People help one another to evolve and grow. So many blocks to growth will be eliminated if the two of you are enhancing each other's growth.

You reinforce your mate when you tell him or her

whenever you see the effort put out and when you share your appreciation of this. Feedback such as this is so encouraging and supportive at a time when changes are intruding into the old illusions. Everyone grieves at the loss of the familiar, and support is reassuring.

Fears also will arise with change, and encouraging your spouse to bring those feelings up and share them, plus your communicating your own fears, will alleviate some of their potency and make them more manageable. It is a lucky pair who faces their fears together. Fears tend to disappear and the couple begins to feel that they can handle anything. Facing fears actually strengthens the relationship.

Sit down together and each make a list of ten fears you experience. Then compare the lists, checking for similarities, differences, trends or particular problem areas. Then talk with each other about those fears, (1) correcting misconceptions, (2) planning ways to deal with the situation involved, (3) imagining the **worst possible consequence** associated with each fear, such as death, an affair, divorce, (4) discovering how this is attached to past fears, and (5) separating what is **imagined** from what is **fact** about the fear.

Fact is what you can know with your five senses, i.e., "I heard ... I saw ... I touched ..." to this we add our own imagination. We interpret and evaluate what this means and then we usually react to our interpretations rather than to the facts. Often the interpretations and evaluations we created in our imaginations are 180 degrees off target and our fear has been for nothing. This is why it is important to check with the spouse.

Lydia went to the show with several associates from work. She called home and told Marvin that she, Freddie, Billie and Jane were going and that she'd be home around 10:00 p.m. Marvin was jealous. He imagined she was having a date, that she didn't care for him, that she'd been having an affair and on and on.

When Lydia came home, happy and relaxed, she was met at the door by Marvin livid with anger, his fear carefully buried, who said, "Well, did you have fun with your boy friend?" She looked confused and stunned, then began to laugh, and then said, "Freddie and Billie are **girl** friends I work with; I told you about their being at the company picnic with their children. I see your eyes flashing fire and you're red-faced. I'm feeling afraid and yet I'm bursting with laughter about the mix-up."

The humor enabled this incident to be easily straightened out, but how much pain could have been avoided if Marvin had waited to check out the facts instead of reacting to his imagination. He needed this feedback.

The most useful feedback is a description of your mate's behavior rather than an inference about the underlying motivation. Then report how you experience this behavior, this way giving information about both your mate and about you. Marsha told James, "I see your mouth held in tightly and you are turning away from me. I feel confused and afraid you are angry with me." A good example of honest feedback.

Some productive rules to follow are: Avoid making interpretations. Tell what you feel and what you experience. Tell your mate the affect he or she is having on you. Do not tell your partner what is going on inside him or her.

Don't say, "You're mad at me and you think I was out playing around," or "You're just jealous because you want to go out and have an affair yourself."

Interpretations are often projections, i.e., we see the other person in the light of our own dynamics. What we have going on inside us we think is going on with our partner. A good way of checking this out is the following: If you interpret something about another person, then say the exact same thing about yourself and see if it fits; see if it is a projection of your feelings. You might say to yourself, "I'm just jealous because I want to go out and play around myself." If it feels familiar and seems to fit, share this with your spouse. In this particular instance, it might provide information that will promote the two of you into discovering new ways to make your sex life better so you will not be looking for excitement out there instead of right here.

In this Happiness Bubble you will find a strong tendency to evaluate your progress by others' opinions, statements and evaluations. If Mom says, "You two certainly are getting along well and you seem so happy doing everything together. I'm glad that you don't fight like other couples do." You may tend to discount the upset stomach you have every day along with the feelings of anger, mostly hidden, that are insistently attempting to communicate to you the dissatisfaction with the state of your relationship.

Checking your satisfaction level provides more accurate information than listening to what other people think. For a week each night when you go to bed, check the calendar with a symbol that records whether you felt mostly happy and satisfied or mostly full of pain and dissatisfied today.

S satisfied D dissatisfied

SUN.	MON.	TUES.	WEDS.	THUR.	FRI.	SAT.
D	D	S	D	D	S	D

Results: 5 D's and 2 S's.

Something needs attention!

Ask yourself, "How much time do I spend thinking about how my partner needs to change?" We do not have the power nor the right to try to change others. We can change ourselves and thereby improve the relationship, or we can ask for what we need from our partner. Then allow him or her to choose whether or not to make changes. The issue here is whether or not the force of our energy is on our mate changing or on our taking charge and creating a satisfactory relationship -- becoming the master rather than the victim. You cannot change the entire relationship but you are creating 50% of it and that's quite an influential proportion.

Check out your illusion level. Do you still have an idea of how it is supposed to be? Are you still trying to get it to be the dream marriage you know it should be, rather than letting it be what it is naturally? Are your dreams about the perfect mate and what it would take for your spouse to be like that? Are your thoughts of the future rather than the present? "When John learns to ... If only he'd ... Someday when we get our new house... If she'd lose weight..."

If you find your illusion level too high, you can practice seeing your situation as it is rather than what it should be. This is acceptance, the basic building block for an effective relationship.

Begin by using your five senses, looking around you, stating "I see John reading in his favorite easy chair, I smell the food cooking in the kitchen. I hear the radio playing. I feel the soft carpet under my feet. I feel the 'uptightness' in my stomach begin to diminish. I feel caring as I see John look up and say, 'Is dinner about ready?' "

This exercise will connect you to the present -- where life truly is. So much wasted energy is focused on hurts and regrets of the past, or hopes and fears about the future. In order to be married and be progressing through its stages with joy and pleasure, you need to consciously be here now. So put down the past and future and be present in your marriage as you advance on to the next stage.

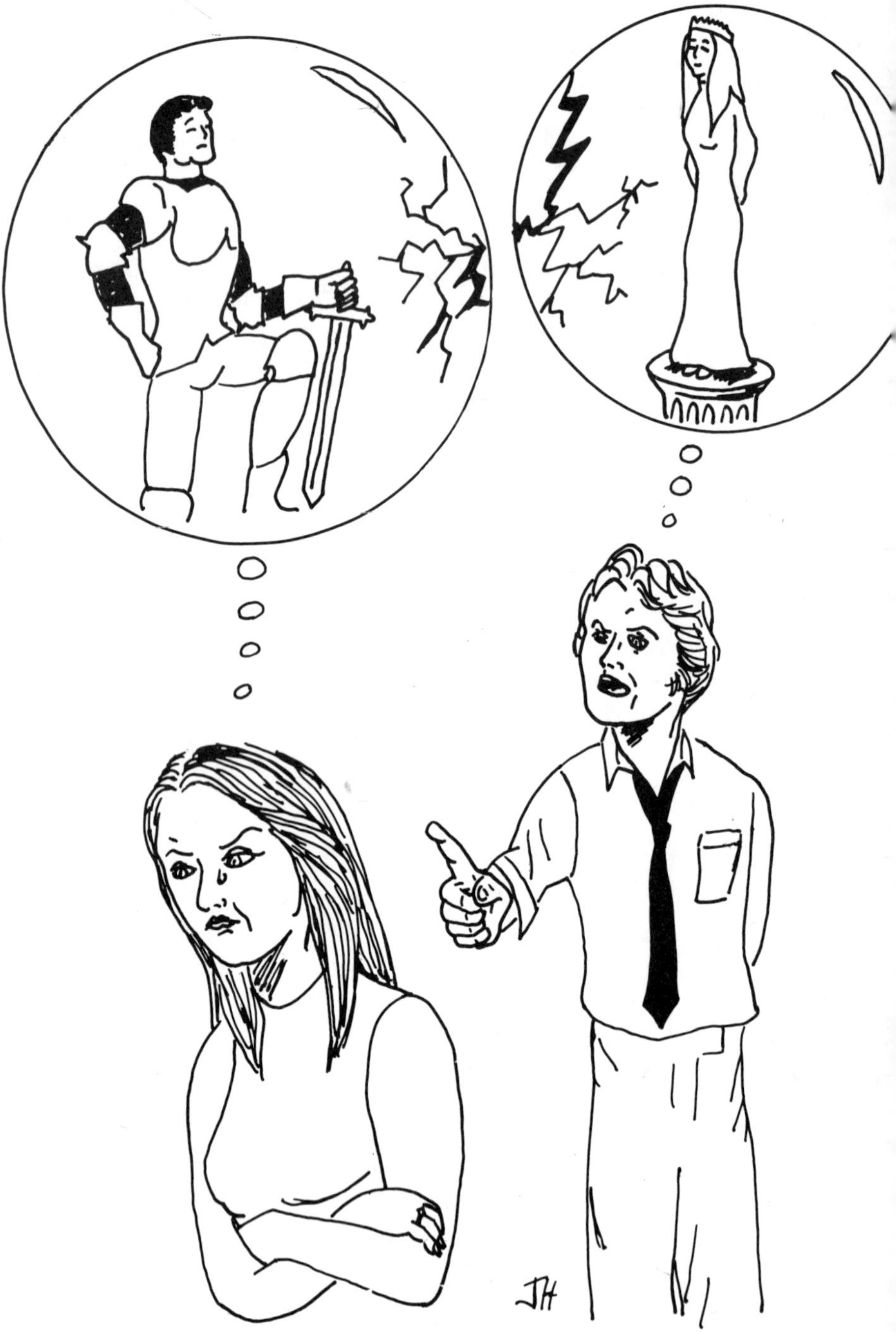
JH

V
BURSTING THE BUBBLE, STAGE 2

Identifying the stage

In the previous chapter, the Happiness Bubble we alluded to a person split in half, the disowned half and the fantasy half. The fantasy half dominated the initial stage of marriage, always putting the best forward and carefully hiding any character flaw that might disenchant the partner.

Now the disowned half comes pushing into dominance in this stage we call Bursting the Bubble. Not only is the fantasy bubble gone, but the bursting action is loud and dramatic -- evident in the fighting and power struggling going on now. Bursting the Bubble is remembering the fantasy and being angry with the partner for not fulfilling your dream. If you are experiencing this, your Bubble is Bursting.

The characteristic feeling of this stage is anger, covering hurt and disappointment. This may be expressed as depression because depression is anger turned inward. But usually the action is blaming either your partner or yourself for being the cause of the disappointment. It is easy to slip from the stage one fantasy into this stage by becoming disillusioned with one aspect at a time and blaming the partner each time for not fulfilling your expectations.

A young man sat in the office with his hands and teeth clenched. His story is fairly typical. His wife had led him to believe that she would be his showpiece, entertaining his business associates and presenting her best foot forward in style. When she began to gain weight and dress dowdily, the young man became angry and began blaming her for any normal slump in his business activities. He focused on her rather on the problems at hand. She countered by withholding sex and then he countered that by spending more time at the office. It became a situation that he saw as "all her fault."

Although this story shows many dynamics at play, it depicts most clearly a gradual slipping from "fairy princess" to "old hag."

The second aspect of blaming is blaming yourself. We say, "If I were just more adequate, the dreams would come true. If I just tried harder ..." Self-blaming is just as unfair. The payoff of blaming yourself instead of the partner is that you never have to bring the problem into the open. The inadequate one can suffer in the silence of self-degradation and never let the problems surface for discussion and possible resolution.

The self-blamer says, "What's the matter with me that this isn't working out," and the pointer-blamer says, "What's the matter with you?" What's the matter lies in the illusion about the relationship.

Blaming only creates a battle and does not solve anything.

Behavior can become irrational in this stage because of the misguided attempt to manage and control the relationship. The behavior is not working. A common method of handling this is to intensify or increase such behavior. For instance, she may say to herself, "If I'm letting him know about my anger by arriving home late from work and I think he's not hearing me, I'll get later and later until one day I just won't come home at all. Then he'll be sorry." A useful rule to follow is if something is not working, stop it. Do something, anything, different, but don't keep doing what does not work.

At this point some couples give up. They are so afraid of divorce that they resign themselves to the situation and continue on sometimes for years with a barely recognized, low-level depression of disappointment and pain. They still half-way attempt to keep the old illusions alive -- an impossible job when one has seen the reality of it all. They cannot see anything ahead worth fighting for, so they deny the anger, fear and pain. This resignation has stifled the possiblities for growth of each individual and of the relationship.

However the illusion is gone. Anger appears either as a looming, quiet depression or a loud angry cry. If you are caught in one of these behavior cycles, your Bubble is Bursting.

Theoretical perspectives

Psychological theorists have much to say about this stage. Erik Erikson describes it in terms of a confused two-year-old. It is easy to picture a stocky toddler blaming his rocking horse for making him fall when it is really his inexperienced coordination at work. The goal of the tyke is autonomy, freedom from Mommy.

If this marriage has a parent-child style of interaction between thc couple, one eventually will have to chafe under the bit of his or her role because, as adults, it is uncomfortable to be in either the parent or the child role to another adult. People are striving for autonomy ... to be themselves. Like the toddler learning about his world, the couple is learning about the relationship.

An example of a parent-child style of interaction is portrayed like this: The husband asks permission to play poker with the boys, just as a youngster asks permission from Mommy to cross the street or the wife asks permission of the husband to buy a new dress. The key words are "ask permission."

Another example involves parental sanction, i.e., the husband would disapprove if the wife's skirt was too short or if she talked loudly in public. Or the wife would frown to chastise the husband for saying "shit" in front of the children or would coyly flirt with him to persuade him to do or buy something. There are no adults here, just parents and children.

Since most marriages begin with the premise that husband knows about money, cars, sex and the world, and wives are experts on homemaking, babies, typing and general family organization, it is easy for him to always be Papa, even to Mama. With the addition of current changes in day care. Mama's full-time job, professional career and birth control, the husband and wife roles are confused. However, whose responsibility is it to see that supper is served? Even if he helps or starts supper, it is still seen ultimately as her task since she is the expert.

It is easier to see the role imposition when the wife stomps her liberated foot and says, "Dinner's your responsibility this week," than it is to see the man telling Mama that he has made "plans with friends for the evening, so don't wait up." The story is the same though. Each person is seeking the autonomy from being "parented" by the spouse.

Autonomy from the partner does not mean the irresponsibility of extra-marital sex with flagrant disrespect for another's values. It means beginning with the understanding that, in the U.S.A., one adult need NOT seek permission to be away from home, especially for only a few hours, from another adult.

Freud sees the second stage of individual development as anal (issues of withholding or not withholding) exemplified by toilet training. The toddler exhibits complete control of his situation because only he can choose to give those bowel movements to Mom and the potty. The second stage of work in a relationship then is "How much control do I claim? What is the trade-off? How do I figure out what to give for what I want in return?"

Maslow says that after a person has seen to the meeting of his bodily needs, next are his safety needs. "How can I feel safe? Do I need to lock the door? Do I need to keep that mistake a secret to feel safe in my mate's presence and gain approval? What companions do I want around me? Can I feel safe from having items stolen, secrets told, being embarrassed, from being imprisoned in a clutching relationship?" When you ask your mate to be dependent on you, he or she struggles like a two-year old, to release himself from the unsafe trapped feelings of inferiority this generates.

William Schutz defines the second stage of his life cycle in interpersonal development in terms of control behavior where one party seeks to mold the behavior of another through influence, coersion, ordering or persuasion. He even breaks control behavior down into (1) what we want to do to others, and (2) what we want other to do to us. Stage 2 is chuck full of control struggles.

Elizabeth Kuhbler-Ross calls the second stage of grieving the anger stage, citing the usual reaction is "Why me?" Today we recognize that we not only grieve over death but the loss of anything important -- such as, a job, spouse, income status, or hopes and dreams. For instance, grief over something other than death is a retired man who grieves over the loss of working because it met so many of his needs.

The marriage partner grieves over the lost fantasy, the honeymoon bliss. He or she may feel that the marriage, or the spouse, is less than ideal and is withholding this bliss. Feeling cheated definitely is anger-producing material. Anger covers the hurt of being disillusioned.

Anger, then, is the subject of many writings. Since anger expressed or unexpressed is such a basic part of the Bursting Bubble and is such an intense emotion, it affects every facet of one's life, especially the life with a partner.

Sex

Behold the battle field! If one partner wanted to show anger at the other, the most powerful way seems to be to deny sex. People say, "How can I make love to someone at whom I'm so angry." Since sex is viewed as a human's most intimate behavior, "Who wants to be intimate with the louse who embarrassed me tonight?" Some partners just turn over to go to sleep.

Sex during the Bursting of the Bubble stage is sparse and rigid at times. The effect is self-perpetuating when "no sex tonight" becomes anger-producing material to use against the spouse later.

Without the fantasy that sex always is magic and euphoric, the couple begins to feel left out, cheated of what is rightfully his or hers according to the dream, a full sex life.

The facet of marriage not presented in the "American Ideal" is that learning and experimentation are involved in sex. It is just supposed to happen. The virgin bride instantly becomes a vamp with the mere addition of an exciting husband and he always knows what to do to make it wonderful. Couples don't automatically know everything but they are supposed to create a magnificent moment that will continue always.

The truth is that trust and acceptance are the foundation for any real intimacy shared in the bedroom. Acceptance that they neither one know everything. Trust that either can say, "No Honey, I'm tired tonight." This is not usually present at this stage. Here in the Bursting of the Bubble the "No, Honey" becomes a withholding tactic. Sadly, it is almost impossible to have trust and acceptance in this stage.

Social situation

Because sexual needs seldom are met by the spouse in this stage, the social scene becomes a place of tension -- sometimes reflected in sex games. Light flirting, suggestive jokes and drinking usually tell the story of frustrated anger and sexual neglect. Cocktail parties are full of angry people.

Two disillusioned and angry individuals respond to each other in society in several typical ways. The most obvious is public insulting, a sense of humor designed to humiliate. Some people use insults on others to show their basic anger at humanity. Others, however, use of the jibe as a tool in public to humiliate the spouse. One wife would quietly take a confidant aside to complain about her husband's behavior, behind his back, while the husband complains about his wife in the locker room. Each is seeking support for their pain and argue that he or she has been wronged and is justified in being angry. Other couples can act lovey-dovey in public and scream out all their anger behind the bedroom door. Some couples maintain cool distance.

The anger from the Bursting of the Bubble is acted out in different ways by different couples in the social situation.

Children and household duties

Household duties receive more attention in this

stage than any other. The partners are focusing anger on unwashed dishes, unmade beds and picking up socks instead of the real issue of the unfulfilled fantasy. While in stage one, the little woman loved to care for her husband. Now she feels used and taken advantage of. She begins to say, "I could be replaced by a dishwasher and he'd be just as happy." Remember that this feeling seems to be confirmed by the limited sexual proof of devotion.

The husband begins to think, "My Mom always ironed my socks. Mary led me to believe she just loved to iron my socks, too. Why all the hassle now?" He also is feeling sexually deprived and sees Mary as withholding not only sex but services assumed to be in the unspoken contract of "perfect wife, perfect husband."

Sometimes the reverse is true. In response to her suggestion for more attention and help, he tries to help in the kitchen or the laundry, but she corrects him and makes fun of his bumbling efforts until he stops trying. She secretly feels that if he tries to start supper, it implies that she is inadequate for not having started supper yet. So his attempts carry messages of hurt and inadequacy according to her interpretation, whether he means it or not. So she blocks the very help she needs.

She holds no corner on the market of confusion,

many men feel put down if the wife tries to help by mowing the lawn or attempting to fix a faucet. Inside he receives the message, "You didn't do your job, so I'll have to do it," when she may be just saying, "I'd like to help."

The various misunderstandings add pressure as this couple faces the fact that the fantasy is over. Real issues of disappointment and unfulfilled expectations are under all those arguments about dishes and socks. To focus on the house, lets off steam without turning the fire off under the pot, or getting to the real problem.

But, to focus on children can build up more steam than it lets off. The American Ideal for Parenthood requires that we be patient and loving parents at all times. This strains any person, let alone an angry, neglected person. In many families, the children (at least the first child) came along while the Happiness Bubble was intact. All the excitement of a new baby and parenthood seemed to complete the perfect picture of a happy family that was living up to the promise of this American Ideal.

With the Bursting of the Bubble this perfect picture could no longer be preserved. The anger comes out everywhere. The extreme of angry parent's behavior to children is child abuse. It is not the uncaring parent who abuses the child but the angry caring parent. The angry parent sees the child as (1) overpowering and in control, (2) always taking and never giving, (3) withholding obedience on purpose to be stubborn and (4) a never-ending problem. Children feel insecure around angry people and their insecurity makes them controlling, grasping and disobedient.

Presupposing that the child clearly understands what is expected, he or she will try to comply if someone will notice and give strokes, or if he or she doesn't fear the rejection of the parent. Notice how much like big people children are. Some people rightfully refer to them as "little people." But they don't hide feelings very well. They have not learned how yet.

Let us say quickly that the difficult behavior of the child is **not** totally dependent on the behavior of the parents. The stubborn two-year-old is growing and wants to evaluate and participate in life as he or she sees it. A two-year-old must struggle for autonomy and say "No" to everything to pass beyond this stage on the road to maturity and adulthood. This kind of behavior would not be so common if it did not serve some purpose. Incidentally, observe the similarity between the two-year-old behavior and that of the angry spouse. Both feel unfulfilled, afraid and out of control.

The most prevalent aspect of the parent-child relationship at this stage is control. While the partners battle for control of the fantasy and each other, either with fighting or manipulation, the parents use the same techniques on the children to gain control. The child's growth toward being an independent person is seen as a challenge to parental authority and a rejection of the parent's love and sacrifices.

The stereotypic example of this battle is seen between parents and the first adolescent. Research may prove that delinquent adolescents have parents who are locked in this second stage of marriage, if the parents made it this far. In this scene, everyone feels misunderstood, taken advantage of and hurt. Everyone seems to be inhibiting the growth of everyone else. Worse yet, no one seems to be able to say, "I'm hurt because of this ..." or discuss anything. Emotions run at a fever pitch and many families shatter. This is not necessary. The solution, in part, rests on communication, the focus of the next topic.

Communication

As we have shown, Bursting of the Bubble is full of miscommunication with misunderstanding as a direct result. Most verbage starts with "You ..." It goes something like, "You didn't mow the lawn, You never understand me, You are an unattentive partner, You are a disobedient child." Basically all the previous sentences communicate, "You are inadequate." Notice that there is no mention of the speaker's feelings, desires or expectations. If all of your messages are "You" messages such as these, you're in stage two and angry as hell.

Since the communication here is so muddied, even simple things become distorted. For instance, if a man plays golf in stage one, it usually is because he sees golf as a business contact bringing prestige and a socially permitted time without spouse. However, in stage two when the Bubble has Burst, playing golf can be height of manipulation where he goes away to play for hours at a time, leaving her to clean house or tend baby. He is non-verbally communicating, "I'm angry and don't want to be with you." American women have yet to create so versatile and acceptable style of avoidance.

Whole volumes of literature have discussed communication and each one deals with the straightening out of crooked lines of communication. While most of these are verbal, the body communicates much. In this stage stomach and bowel disorders come to the surface. The body reflects tension through headaches, hemorrhoids, diarrhea, knotted stomach muscles and ulcers. If you pay attention to your body, you can listen to its messages. A client reported once that his stomach felt more relaxed than in years after a particularly angry fight with his wife during which he said what

REALLY was bothering him. He talked it out so his body did not have to act it out.

The problem for many people in this stage is their unwillingness to face the fear inside that the spouse will get angry and go away forever. Many stage two partners cannot be secure enough to say, "This isn't right and I want to work it out. But if I tell you that I'm concerned about our marriage, you might go away and give up on me." As a result, the words, thoughts and deeds reflect the anger pent up inside in an unclear, attacking verbal barrage.

The actions of an angry partner many times communicate more than words. Knowing what your partner does NOT like can give you weapons to use against him or her that will push buttons and stimulate an angry reaction. If she knows that he doesn't like to wait, she may deliberately be late or even "forget" the time. Consciously or unconsciously, she stimulates his anger and expresses her anger at him. He may "forget" their anniversary knowing that a remembrance is important to her.

Many writers have shouted the merits of communication as a panacea to all of society's problems. This may be an overstatement but straightening out our communication can always help and verbalizing our anger can take a load off our minds and our stomach.

Work and play

The angry employee probably has caused more sick days, slowdowns and errors than all the machinery and computers put together. Or on the other hand, the angry employee can be an industrious worker, spending most of his or her waking hours at work instead of home. Or the angry employee can be unemployed chronically, communicating anger by being unable to remain on a job. In any case the angry employee is a problem in the work-a-day world.

The free-from-anger employee gives full attention for the required number of hours and then goes home to rest and recharge his or her battery. If home cannot provide rest and the required recharge, the attention that should be paid to the job is not focused on the business at hand and can cause errors, delays and even injuries. The company nurse treats far more cases of "personal problems" than industrial injuries. The concerned nurse refers her patients to a social worker or psychiatrist and encourages the company to aid a good employee to straighten out his or her affairs.

An angry husband can spend more and more hours at the office or on the road. An angry wife can spend hours at her own work or continuously talk about it at home. A complaint one husband voiced was that his wife was either on the job or always talking about it. He was pleased that she enjoyed her work and felt stimulated by it, but he really was sick of her discussing nothing else. Underneath he was saying that it made him feel as if he could not capture his wife's interest as her job could. Underneath she was feeling afraid to discuss real problems at home because he might find out about her disappointment in the marriage and maybe give up and leave.

Much job frustration occurs when a partner is in stage two where there is so much anger. The cycle produced possibly looks like this: He is angry because he is disappointed that the marriage is not perfect, so he goes to work angry and worried. At work he makes mistakes, gets stomach aches and bawls out an employee or two. Because of those things, his boss "talks" to him and he goes home angry that the company does not understand how much he gives them and how much he cares. At home again, his wife might advise him to keep his temper and take some more stomach medicine while she mixes him a drink. The message she conveys is that his problems at work are not what she wants to spend time discussing and, again, he has no place to talk about his real anger, but it has to stay inside ready to be acted out at work tomorrow. What a bind!

If a husband's anger is displayed by working long he accomplishes several goals: (1) he gets back at his wife for not being the ideal he married, (2) he shows the boss that he is a hard worker and deserves a promotion or raise, and (3) he successfully avoids dealing with the family problems, car troubles, raising kids, fixing a leaky roof or resolving his anger. So when the roof is leaky and he must work on Saturday, his wife has to manage the home by herself (after all, that's her job) and see that the roof is fixed. This adds to her anger and feelings of disappointment. Even more anger-producing for her, however, is the ever present thought that her profession is neglected by having to be an at-home mother and wife.

Wives who work out of the home may have a different focus for their anger. She may say to herself, "Why do I have to work all day long and then come home and take care of everything? He was supposed to help me and make my life happy instead I don't get anything." No matter what the specific work arrangement it seems no one in stage 2 is happy with the situation as it is.

Even with the issue of play, no one is happy or is having any fun. Where we go, what we will do, who we will be with are all arenas for fights. There is usually a feeling of confusion inside because in the Happiness Bubble, everything was done together and they enjoyed it so much. Now nothing's right or fun anymore and neither party understands what happened.

The only consistent thing is that members are quite unhappy much of the time and generally uncomfortable all of the time because of all the unspoken and unfocused anger.

Self-concept

"I must be doing something wrong. If I only were more secure, I wouldn't let this bother me. I must not deserve any better and, after all, I'm lucky he (or she) is not running around on me or, worse, leaving me." This illustrates how a person feels as the Bubble Bursts and problems arise. Self-esteem is low at this point and the self-concept is shaky. The higher a person's self-esteem, the shorter the time he or she will spend in stage two. "If I think I deserve a better deal than the one I'm getting, I'll arrange in a hurry to either straighten it out or get out so that I can be comfortable."

"However, if I believe that this is all I deserve, or that I'm powerless to change the situation, I could stay here forever." Some individuals do not realize that life need not hurt every day. Many people, because of their own upbringing, believe that only one kind of marriage is possible -- like that of their parents. Others want to avoid the marriage they saw at home but do not know how to be different.

If a girl learns from watching Mama that men can be manipulated by flirting, being coy, seeming stupid and dependent and that this is the only way to be a wife, how could she know to claim her strong points and communicate candidly? She comes away thinking that she didn't develop her skills at getting him to take care of her well enough.

Positive regard and respect for one's self is the key to progressing through the anger stage as quickly as possible. If you thrust yourself to meet your own needs when the spouse fails to do so, your self-confidence and self-esteem will grow creating a better self-concept. You feel pleased that you can take over and do the job yourself, thereby propelling yourself into the next stage, Self-Discovery.

Techniques and tools

How to find the feelings and fears

The techniques included in this chapter will deal with how to survive and get through this stage as an individual and as a partnership. Stage 2 is the funnel to the divorce court usually. Bitter and angry recriminations ring out and sometimes one person storms out in anger. The marriage seems unsalvageable. You NEVER could say everything you have saved up to say. Counseling often is seen as inappropriate by partners who just want away from the feeling of being trapped in the relationship. Some partners have been angry so long that they do not see how a positive relationship could come from all that emotional turmoil.

Answering the following set of questions can help you decide if you are here in stage two:

1. Do you feel that your spouse will never understand you?
2. Do you feel that if your partner just knew who you really are that he or she would hate, disrespect you or leave?
3. Are you afraid of spending time alone and fear you'll never feel close in your marriage?
4. Do you feel that your spouse is uniquely at fault and imperfect?
5. Do you feel that you are doing the lion's share of the compromising and giving in?

If you answer yes to most of the above questions, your feelings may be summarized in the following list:

misunderstood, vulnerable, lonely and alone, angry, used, disappointed, hurt, anxious, and afraid.

Resentment is definitely present also. This resentment needs to be released or it will hurt you. Just like the man carrying some acid around in his hand, others notice it and may be surprised and feel bad for a moment, but he is the one who is going to be hurt by it. A potent tool for the resentment and anger of stage two is to practice forgiving. Use this affirmation several times a day:

"I fully and freely forgive __________, and I release you to do your best."

Do this also for yourself:

"I fully and freely forgive myself, and I release me to do my best."

Another way to discover what your feelings and fears are is to say each of the following sentences to yourself with your eyes closed and see if any sentence fits for you.

I feel nobody will ever understand me.

I feel my spouse would judge me unworthy if he or she knew ...

I feel I'll have to fill my own time and be my own company not because I choose but because no one else wants me.

I feel cheated out of a caring partner.

I feel I'll give up all I really want and need to preserve this marriage.

By bringing the feelings and fears to our attention, we can decide what to do about them. We do not have to let them just take over pushing us into angry outbursts that are unproductive.

How to change your attitude

We choose what we think and feel. We can change our feelings just as we can change our mind, our thinking, our attitude. One technique to change your attitude is to use the following chart:

A	B	C	D
activating event	your belief system	your consequent feeling and behavior	your challenge or denial of your belief

This is based on Albert Ellis' theory which states that it is your belief system that causes your feelings and behavior, not the events in your life. When someone does something to you, i.e., forgets your birthday, your feelings may get hurt. You often think the other person made you feel bad, or that A, above, caused C. You felt disappointed, unappreciated and angry.

But it actually was B that caused C, your beliefs about the forgetting of your birthday that produced your pain. Your thoughts went something like this: "He doesn't care anymore. If he cared for me, he'd remembered. Daddy always remembered Mom's birthday and I remembered his last month. He just doesn't care." Feelings flow from thoughts and those thoughts produced the pain. In this example it fits into the model like this:

A	B	C	D
Forgotten Birthday	Beliefs and thoughts about it	Painful feelings	Challenge of those thoughts

To utilize D and change the painful situation, you can challenge your belief that he does not care, by checking out his other behavior throughout the day and his telling you about whether or not he cares. You can remind yourself that your marriage is different than your parent's marriage, and that your husband is different than your father. You can remember when you forgot someone's birthday and check inside yourself to see if that meant you did not care for them. You could think, "Birthdays aren't all that important. I know he loves me because of the love in his eyes when he left for work this morning. So what if he forgot." The consequent feelings now would be very different. Your vision had shifted. Once we gain perspective, we can change our hurt feelings to feelings of understanding and patience if we can challenge our belief system and reject the influence we allow a person to have over our feelings.

An excellent technique is called the Karate

Method. When your spouse blames you, don't get defensive and begin arguing. This happens all too often in stage two. Instead, find the part of you that actually does do what your spouse accused you of doing, and say, "Yes, I'm like that when I ..." and then add, "**and** I'm also ..." In the second part of the sentence turn the conversation to a new direction that supports you.

This is what a Karate Master does. He flows with the opponents force and then throws him over. "Yes, I am attacking and harsh to you sometimes I know, **and** I also care about our marriage and want to talk this out so things will be better. I want to hear your pain and want you to hear mine."

Remember don't be defensive. It just fuels the fire. You can only change your attitude, not someone else's. Paradoxically, it works every time that you gain what you are willing to quit worrying about and let happen. It is impossible to make somebody love you, no matter what you do. You can make yourself a valuable housekeeper, servant, sex partner but you cannot make someone love you.

The key is to permit someone, (a fortuante someone), to love you, make love to you, and share life with you as a valuable person. The minute you stop trying to make the partner love you and instead make yourself a loveable person, the spouse is free to really love you. Making oneself loveable is not being accommodating which is giving in to the partner's every whim. You become loveable when you love yourself, and your loveableness radiates to all you meet, including your partner.

How to change your behavior.

There is an old song that says, "I'm going to change my way of talking and if that ain't enough, I'm going to change the way I strut my stuff." This is wisdom being taught to us in a song.

If we change our physical behavior, such as, smiling at others, walking with pride and joy, standing tall, breathing deeply, we will feel better and more confident. Other people will respond to us more favorably. As we make these changes, life just seems to change.

Changing the way we talk is so helpful when the Bubble has Burst. If you have discovered an important new awareness about yourself, share it along with the intensity of this insight for you. "I found out something really interesting about myself and I want to share it with you ..." Choose a time when your spouse can easily pay attention because a statement like that should not have to compete with a TV or screaming infant.

Notice that when you communicate effectively, you will be using "I" messages. "I" messages are sentences beginning with "I want ... I feel ... I need ..." basically stating to your partner how you are feeling at this moment in time, leveling about who you are and what is going on with you. There is no attempt to manipulate or attack the other party. It is simply a statement about you, not the other person, which eliminates the defensive rebuttal that comes when a person feels attacked, as in "You" messages. The sentences were not hidden "You" messages and did NOT say "I found out why **you** are such a bum." The behavior of using "I" messages yourself and setting an example will encourage the partner to give you the same attention.

A technique that is useful and fun to use is to imagine that a part of you is a "Super" person. When you have some behavior that needs changing or some question that needs an answer, ask Super ________ (insert your name) what to do. All of us have the answers inside but we have not effectively learned to turn inward and listen for answers. This works and you will be astounded at the wisdom you already have. (Stop reading and try it now).

How to deal with staying in a stage by choice

You may have decided that, yes, you're in stage two, angry as hell and choose to stay here without trying any new exercises and continue to do what you've always done in the past. The key is that you **decided.** Many couples stay in stage 2 because (1) the displays of anger are few enough to be discounted, (2) the unknown new style is scary, (3) they like the payoff received.

A couple married 25 years finally realized how angry they were at each other and spent the next year trying to deny or change their anger by each being more agreeable. So with few outbursts of anger, they could maintain the system forever. However, this requires alot of energy and effort because growth is natural and inhibiting this growth is hard work. They have chosen a path that will require alot of energy, but it may be more preferable for this couple than facing the next stage.

You may decide to stay here for just a specified length of time, i.e., until Mom dies (trouble would break her heart), or until the children come (because you believe erroneously that children will hold the marriage together), or until the children are grown. Facing the unknown that change would bring is put off until sometime later when the situation is different or until you are strong enough to face it.

The most comfortable reason for staying anywhere is that we receive some reward for doing so. The reward for remaining in the Bursting of the Bubble with all the anger and problems may be confirmation of long-held feelings of unworthiness that, once again, prove that we are not loveable. If we need to feel unworthy badly enough because this is an idea we learned as a child, we will put up with alcoholism, beatings, child abuse, or any number of extremes.

Another prevalent reason for staying in stage 2 is because of a financial payoff. A woman whose long-time husband is financially successful might think twice about rocking the boat, especially if she has no skills to market. Or the partner may be a steady provider and she needs help while she completes her education and becomes established in the work world.

Know that you have decided to stay here and that it is okay to choose to do so. Say to yourself, "I give myself permission to stay right where I am and it's okay." Simply verbalizing to yourself that you give yourself permission to do something is a powerful technique.

Taking charge and choosing is commendable. Only you can know what you need at this time and stage in your marriage, and there is no right and wrong.

How to work with an unwilling partner

Many individuals would like to move on but see the task equal to moving a mountain if they have to drag the partner along. Even a willing partner may be unwilling to examine the marriage as deeply as you, but if you share your new insights, at least the partner will feel included in your thinking and planning.

Usually the unwilling partner is afraid. Afraid to question the situation or move forward to a new stage for fear that the benefits would be lost. Many men will not support a wife who seeks "liberation" because of the fear of loss of service and the relationship that he now considers binding. After all, who cooks dinner in the home of a liberated woman? Many a man fears it will be him.

Some women married because they saw themselves as undesirable to anyone but the spouse. If the spouse begins to move forward and question the relationship, she may be left out in the cold and, consequently, she feels very afraid and unwilling to move to a new stage.

If you want either to encourage your spouse to grow with you or to make your spouse the most comfortable with your growing, you can do one of several things.

You can speak in a straight line, stating honestly what you are really thinking and feeling. State what you dislike, being specific, how it makes you feel, and what adjustment you hope for in response. For example, when your wife arrives late for dinner, say,

"I feel used and taken advantage of. I need you to call me if you're going to be late to keep me from feeling hurt." You have provided all the information necessary to let the partner decide what to do.

Let your life show that growth feels good and is rewarding, but not only when it is congenial. When the struggle is painful, you must let that show too so that an honest picture is presented.

Honest representation of your position (as well as you know it) will encourage the same response. The partner is shown that "We don't have to be afraid of each other," and more importantly, "I'm not out to get you."

The possibility for resolution of anger must be made attractive to the spouse. Who could resist the offer to make life more comfortable? If you approached your spouse by saying, "It's been kind of tense around here lately and I'd sure like to make things better. I'm reading this book that can help me understand what may be going on," you might get a more willing response.

Your spouse may respond by saying, (1) "Tense? What do you mean? I'm not tense, it must be you?" or (2) "What does it say?" or (3) "I want things to be better and I hope it will help." Both 2 and 3 are positive responses. Your handling of response number 1 will tell the tale. You could show your vulnerability by saying, "Yes, I've been feeling tense and would like for us to get along better." Your candor will pay off and show your partner that you are willing to be honest and talk about feelings.

Listening is just as important. If your spouse needs to share an insight while you are making supper, hear him or her out right then. It will be worth it, supper can wait.

If your spouse sees you feeling better, it will make at least your growth attractive, maybe growth in general. We are rewarded by success so if your mate sees you successful, he or she may be encouraged to try. Possibly the fear will be alleviated; it is fear that is underneath an unwilling spouse's resistance to change.

However, you may be reading this book after the breakup of your marriage. You may have a partner who refuses to see you as anything but a stage 1 princess or prince. You may be single and now deciding whether or not to marry, ever. The tools for coping offered in this book may be used in any close one-on-one relationship no matter the legal state. You always will benefit from knowing and communicating your feelings in any relationship anytime.

If you are separated or divorced, you can use the framework to view the progress anyway. Some couples progress onward to remarry and create the best possible marriage because of the time apart. But in any event you are beginning to understand what happened in your marriage. That insight can prevent your making the same mistake again, in this relationship or a future one.

If you are single, you can live through stages 1,2 and 3 before even getting married and be more certain your marriage will last a while once you do. You are just doing the work before going down the aisle. The work is harder if you are not living together, but not impossible if you insist on being candid with each other.

Since the next stage is Self-Discovery, many partners lead a loosely-structured married life as they move into that stage. Some have partners who travel a lot, some return to college or to work. One fellow had a wife that lived in a town 200 miles away while she went back to medical school. He stayed home and tended the children and kept the home together. Almost all relationships change significantly in some fashion as the move to stage 3 is made. Moving on requires a personal commitment to growth whether or not your partner joins you. You cannot make anyone grow with you anymore than you can make someone love you.

How to work with a willing partner

A willing partner is a rare treasure. We human

beings evolve in interaction with one another. Even our natural abilities, such as walking and talking must be encouraged or they do not develop properly. We need one another to grow. Marriage is a marvelous opportunity to help one another with this task of expanding ourselves and becoming more than we could alone. If you have decided to read this book together, for example, and talk about it, each partner, as well as the partnership, will be enriched.

You can reinforce your partner and ask for reinforcement to be provided for in several important ways:

(1) Open your mind to your partner's way of thinking. Don't let anger stand in the way of giving weight to his or her opinion and feelings.

(2) Use reflective listening and delay your response, check out the information you heard and in this way reinforce the partner's desire to share with you. First, reflect back what you heard, then you can give your response.

(3) Set aside a special time to discuss feelings, maybe Friday night with a glass of wine. Treat yourselves as special. It creates a safe atmosphere so anger can be heard.

(4) Let anger be okay in your home. People who yell are just as worthy as people who don't. The way you yell is important; don't hit each other below the belt. Yell your anger but don't attack your mate. It's

the makeup that counts, not how it's done -- but that it **is** done.

Resolution requires honest feedback and we use feedback like a mirror in which we check the image we are portraying of ourself. One example of this is: "I'm really confused by your last sentence. I heard you say you loved me but your eyes flashed and the veins stood out on your neck. Are you mad at me or what?"

When providing feedback to an angry spouse, we must include how we feel and what we heard. "I feel very childish when you point your finger at me and say, 'Don't act just like your Mother.' Could you hold my hand when you talk to me instead?"

Remember it also helps to include how you feel, what your complaint is specifically, and the change you desire. Hopefully, your willing partner also will be trying to include this information.

To evaluate the progress of stage 2, make a list of the major issues confronting you during the Bursting of the Bubble phase in your marriage. The evaluation of each issue brings more progress when in the partner's presence. Discuss how comfortable you are with a given issue. Evaluate each issue on a scale of one to ten, where one equals feeling terrible, ten equals feeling terrific. "On a scale of one to ten, I am at about a three on the issue of discipline with the kids. That's why I want to discuss it."

Go through this evaluation on each issue. It will give you clearer data about what is going on with the two of you and what issues need work. To promote further progress set realistic goals, develop a plan of action for each one, then work to meet these goals.

Any success you can experience in working with your mate will encourage you to fight it through the Bursting Bubble into Self-Discovery.

VI
SELF-DISCOVERY, STAGE 3

Identifying the stage

After Bursting the Bubble, anything's better. Self-Discovery, however, is a whole lot better. Self-Discovery is a three-fold process; (1) to discover who one is, (2) what one needs, and (3) how to meet those needs. In this stage, the person will find out, not figure out, who he or she really is.

Having entered the marriage relationship through fantasy and assumption, and becoming angry over the disappointment of a shattered dream, the individual now turns inward and asks direct questions. Trying out new ways of thinking and new behavior to see if it feels comfortable enough to incorporate in their own personal style is the mode. Behavior in the Self-Discovery state is exemplified by such activities as learning a new skill, going back to school, having an affair, changing careers, changing decor in the home. The person is trying now to find out "who am I" vs. spending more fruitless time on "who others think I am".

The goal of progressing through the Self-Discovery stage is to find out enough about yourself to form a new connection with the spouse at a new level of knowing. This can be accomplished only by becoming acquainted with your needs, learning how to communicate them and learning how to meet them. Essentially, you are taking responsibility for yourself.

The growth and Self-Discovery at this stage is by no means a quick and easy accomplishment. A spouse usually enters stage three saying, "Okay, you S.O.B., if you won't meet my needs, I'll do it myself. I'll show you that I don't need you." Pretty bitter words for someone who is working toward staying married. And Self-Discovery, chaotic as it is, is a necessary part of a continuing successful marriage.

The above message is expressed in the same style as a couple's stage two interaction. If the couple is a fighting and yelling one, the message was probably yelled accompanied by stomping and door slamming. If, however, the anger in stage two was expressed in covert, manipulative ways, the above message probably will not be spoken at all, but just thought about and acted upon.

The partner of a person in the Self-Discovery stage reacts in various, usually intense, ways. It's quite a job to have one's partner suddenly stop fighting and begin to alter his or her life. For example, Sue complains that Fred, suddenly, after much discomfort about his assigned household tasks, decided to take a cooking course at the high school. He asked Sue for a portion of the kitchen for his tools and a set time when he wanted to experiment with his cooking for meals. Sue, obviously confused, felt that Fred was saying that her cooking was inadequate again, in a new way and, consequently, was hurt.

Fred tried to explain that he had two arms and hands, just like Sue, and he would like to learn to cook for himself and for her. Sue's next ploy was to say the kitchen was too small for Fred to have a separate area, and tools for cooking were expensive. This goes on indefinitely. Fred tries to experiment and Sue uses every method she has to keep him the same guy. She's just learning how to manage him after so many fights and does not want him to be changing.

The Self-Discoverer may be very confused, too. Instead of waking up one morning with a different attitude, the Self-Discoverer usually gradually, item by item, feels his or her way about to a new style. Suddenly the partner seems to wake up to a changed person and does not observe the gradual movement. This action accounts for many of the surprise divorces. One morning she says at breakfast, "Look, I've been thinking about things and I've decided to file for divorce. It's not that I don't love you. It's that marriage now is not comfortable for me and I need out." What a breakfast message for the fellow who must hit the commuter bus.

He responds, "Why didn't you tell me you felt that bad? Maybe we can do something about it!" His response is very natural, filled with panic and feelings of failure. Actually, he never knew her well enough to predict her behavior, so the gradual movement to independence was not seen by him, or shared by her. She probably didn't even know the direction her attitude would take her. Her confusion probably was very upsetting, even to her. She tells her friend, "I don't know what's come over me but I'm doing some really crazy things -- like going out after work with friends for a drink. I've never done that. I don't even like liquor."

Some couples know enough about expressing feelings and needs that they develop, mutually, a temporary new life style. The O'Neills' **Open Marriage** tells of one style in great detail. The couple, in effect, contracts for each to go his or her own way for a while, usually while living together. They may give each other permission to have opposite sex friends or even affairs. They may reassign the household routine so that neither cooks but each fends for him or herself. This style is severely complicated and very difficult with pre-school children, so many couples wait until children are at least in school.

The above couple has the highest chance to grow together instead of apart, mainly because the very decisions involved in setting up the new contract require expressions of need and sharing. The other couples cited usually need guidance from a professional to keep them supported through the struggle.

In a nutshell, the Self-Discoverer releases the feelings of responsibility for the partner. She may say, "This partner is a strong person, too, and I don't have to take care of him anymore. He can take care of himself. That means I'm free to take care of myself because I don't want to be dependent on my spouse to take care of me." What a relief!

A person who is learning about himself or herself can be either responsible or irresponsible. If taking care of self means withdrawing the only financial support from several children and didn't help make arrangements for a smoother transition, the Self-Discoverer would be very irresponsible. The responsible person shares the discoveries to the best of his or her ability and takes responsibility, not for the feelings of the other members so much as for the arrangements and logistics for the other members. Many couples use lawyers or friends to help in this.

The Self-Discovery phase accomplishes the final breaking of the child-like symbiotic tie of dependency on the spouse and moving on to a position of self-reliance. This is where one knows oneself, owns all of one's qualities, positive and negative, is aware of needs and develops the initiative to get those needs met.

There is a tremendous backlash of fear in our society with this "I do my thing and you do yours" independency. The fear is that this "me-first" phase will break down marriage totally. The high divorce rate would seem to indicate it. The fact being overlooked is that the divorces are coming about because of the attempt to fit today's human beings into a marriage formula appropriate for people of another mind set who were dependent on each other for raising a family and surviving in that day and age.

We have simply evolved into a new level, a new mind set, with time now for the development of self. Yes, this phase is somewhat selfish as it needs to be for a while, -- just as the adolescent phase is selfish. The Self-Discovery stage is a problem only when one continues in this phase and never moves on. Growth requires movement or there is stagnation and death.

The survival of marriage dictates that the Self-Discoverer positively have this time to learn how to fill his or her own cup so that he or she will have something to give the relationship as new stages emerge, and not be back in the dependency of stage one or two. The dependency is the actual cause of the high divorce rate -- not the caring and self-nurturing of stage three.

The high divorce rate is only a passing phase in the history of marriage due to its growth process. Destruction of old rigid standards is required to construct new, better ways. People have an inner longing for a committed, loving, sharing relationship with a significant other person to share their inner being, to share their life, to marry. Remember our definition of marriage is not the legalized institution of society. It is an emotional commitment between two whole and real people who desire to share their love, their life with each other, be this with or without legal bonds, between male and female, or between homosexual couples. The information provided in the book applies to all instances.

With a willing and communicating partner and a real commitment to the marriage, the Self-Discoverer can stay married and arrive at the stages of more individual and family fulfillment. 1 whole person + 1 whole person = 1 whole marriage. In this stage, Self-Discovery, the focus is on the development of one whole person. Virginia Satir's declaration on self-esteem from the book **Peoplemaking** so aptly fits this stage.

MY DECLARATION OF SELF-ESTEEM

I am me.

In all the world, there is no one else exactly like me. There are persons who have some parts like me, but no one adds up exactly like me. Therefore, everything that comes out of me is authentically mine because I alone chose it.

I own everything about me -- my body, including everything it does; my mind, including all its thoughts and ideas; my eyes, including the images of all they behold; my feelings, whatever they may be -- and all the words that come out of it, polite, sweet or rough, correct or incorrect; my voice, loud or soft; and all my actions, whether they be to others or to myself.

I own my fantasies, my dreams, my hopes, my fears.

I own all my triumphs and successes, all my failures and mistakes.

Because I own all of me, I can become intimately acquainted with me. By so doing I can love me and be friendly with me in all my parts. I can then make it possible for all of me to work in my best interests.

I know there are aspects about myself that puzzle me, and other aspects that I do not know. But as long as I am friendly and loving to myself, I can courageously and hopefully look for the solutions to the puzzles and for ways to find out more about me.

However I look and sound, whatever I say and do, and whatever I think and feel at a given moment in time is me. This is authentic and represents where I am at that moment in time.

When I review later how I looked and sounded, what I said and did, and how I thought and felt, some parts may turn out to be unfitting. I can discard that which is unfitting, and keep that which proved fitting, and invent something new for that which I discarded.

I can see, hear, feel, think, say, and do. I have the tools to survive, to be close to others, to be productive, and to make sense and order out of the world of people and things outside of me.

I own me, and therefore I can engineer me.

I am me and I am okay.

Theoretical perspectives

Erik Erikson describes the third stage of the development of a child's psychosocial skills as a battle between "initiative vs. guilt." The child spends his or her time from age three to five exploring and practicing new behavior. Many times the new behavior is not accepted and approved by our society and the child feels guilty for "doing bad."

The Self-Discovering partner is very much the exploree and experimenter. He or she asks "Can I make it through college at my age? Is blue really enough my favorite color to redecorate the kitchen in it?" etc. The fear of the Self-Discoverer is that he or she will "do bad", in adult terms, FAIL.

Freud describes this stage as oedipal. Simply stated, the child has fantasies about a sexual relationship (not intercourse) with his or her opposite sex parent and feels guilty if he or she fantasizes success. Although a sexual relationship to a child means something entirely different from that of an adult, the goal for both is affection, touching and a power position in the family like "Mommy" or "Daddy". A male child may fantasize that he kills off Daddy so he can marry Mommy, then feels guilty about killing off, even in fantasy, the beloved Daddy. The adult knows the difference between fantasy and reality. The adult attempts to "kill off" the influence of the parent so that he or she can assume the role of an adult.

For example, Judy married Joe because he was so much like her handsome and successful father. She spent her manipulations trying to keep Joe in Daddy's mold and make them alike. When Joe talked about exercise, Judy suggested that Daddy would teach Joe to play golf if he asked. When Joe expressed satisfaction over a task well done, Judy thought of how proud her Dad would be of her for picking such a gem of a fellow. Judy wore pink often because she assumed all men like ladies in pink -- just as her father did.

When Judy entered the Self-Discovery stage, she was surprised to learn that Joe preferred her in yellow but that she preferred herself in green. Notice, no pink. Judy found that Joe enjoyed jogging and kept himself in condition without spending hours away from home, as most golfers do. Judy found that she was proud of Joe for being different from Daddy in some respects. Judy began to relate to Joe as if he were Joe -- not Daddy.

From the oedipal resolution, the growing child moves to finding their place on the see-saw of "industry" (how many cookies can I have, how many baseball cards, how high the grades) -vs- "inferiority" ("If I can't beat somebody, I'm no good."). Couples ask the same questions of one another. "How much money can I have? How many pairs of shoes? How high an allowance?" vs. "If you don't give me this many, you don't love me." In this stage Erikson says, the individual values himself and everything around in terms of quantity.

The next stage for the child is what Freud called Adolescence. The partners in Self-Discovery act very adolescent. Erikson claims that adolescence is the resolution between "who I am" vs. "who others think I am". This same information is sought by the Self-Discovering partners, relevant to the relationship. "Who am I in this relationship? What does my spouse think of me? Am I really like that?" The information gained by asking these questions provides the vital raw data required for mature functioning of the relationship and for the intimate functioning of the individual.

William Schutz describes the behavior in this stage as affection-oriented, where we seek to give and receive, behavior toward us that demonstrates affection in an amount and style that is psychologically comfortable. Where in the stage Bursting the Bubble, sex was sparse and rigid, in Self-Discovery, many partners discover their sexual preferences and needs just as their other preferences and needs. The stage three couple can "make up" after all that fighting and feel free to demonstrate love and caring without feeling as if they are giving ground to do it.

Although affection behavior and sexual expression are different, the connection is made, even by their children, when they see Mommy and Daddy kissing and otherwise expressing affection. What person, no matter what age, wouldn't value expressions of tenderness, approval and desire.

After a person has met his needs for physiological comforts and safety, Abraham Maslow states that the next need to tackle is the need to love and be loved. We seek a sense of belonging with someone, a connection to a special one, to a group. More importantly, we seek to love ourselves, be nurturing to ourselves in our minds and choices. When we treat ourselves as if we were our loving friend, we can get to know a real unique person.

Elizabeth Kuhbler-Ross, in studying the grief process, calls her third stage Bargaining where the grieving person makes deals like "Look God, I'll be a good person if you'll just make me well." The grieving Self-Discoverer says, "Look partner, I'll be a good spouse if you'll just leave me this chunk of my identity, my freedom." The behavior plays out that if he will help her by getting dinner so she can attend an evening class, she will continue living with him while she finishes college.

Partners in the Self-Discovery phase, like children in all developmental models experiment with new behavior and ways of relating. They find some psychologically comfortable and some not. They adopt some new facets of the personality and toss away others. The stage is marked by fluctuating states of comfort as new ideas are tried.

When a person, like Shirley, begins doing more for herself that **she** wants to do, as opposed to doing what others want or think should be done, often overwhelming guilt and fear are experienced. She is caught in the state of "child consciousness." As a child, when experiencing the pleasure of doing what she wanted, she was reprimanded by her parents, i.e., "Don't eat that sugar, it's bad for you and will make you sick." "Don't play so close to the street." "Come here, be careful of that doggie." "Stop eating that cookie, you'll spoil your dinner." Parental prohibitions were attached to the experience of pleasure.

Awareness of this dynamic process enables Self-Discoverers to cope with the fear easier and to keep it from immobilizing their growth. Because of the ebb and flow of the comfort level, the surrounding environment -- family, social group, etc. -- is affected sometimes in dramatic ways as the individual struggles to find a middle ground of comfort in relating.

Sex

The sex life of the Self-Discoverer usually begins

shyly with small tentative feelers toward the partner and new behavior in the bedroom. Most couples come to the marriage bed uneducated about their **own** sexual experiences, let alone those of their partners. The Self-Discoverer may be reading **Fear of Flying** or **The Joy of Sex** for the first time and permitting the imagination to influence his or her actions. A Self-Discovery couple can try new sexual behavior without the fear of being seen as "bad" or "not respectable". The growing person learns, in stage three, that the greatest sexual organ is the brain. Since this Self-Discovery stage is "brain-work"time, in every area, the brain work on sex falls right into place.

The conversation in bed progresses from "If you don't like me to do this, just say so. I've been so angry with you in the past that I don't care if you reject my experiments," to "I trust you to tell me if you don't like my experiments so that I can try to please both of us." As the first tentative feelers are extended and the reception observed, the rest of the behavior will follow from the initial experiments if there is some trust and acceptance.

When new sex behavior is met with disapproval, anger or hurting, the Self-Discoverer may consider having an affair. The newly-selected affair mate may meet the need for the Self-Discoverer to play, to experiment, to be approved. With the affair mate, the Self-Discoverer can giggle, try novel sex and bed experiments and generally feel free from social and marital disapproval. Consider this situation risky, however, because most mates will not tolerate outside sexual relationships easily. The price may be too great.

The more shy Self-Discoverer may have an imaginary affair or perfect masturbating. In the imagination, he or she can experiment with new sex, group sex, gay sex and any new thought without fear of disapproval. Whether imaginary or real, however, he or she searches for an environment that is accepting and secure against the onslaughts of disrespecting influence in which to try new thinking and behavior to see what feels right.

Social situation

The social situation may change drastically as the Self-Discoverer feels less and less comfortable with his or her peers. Each may choose new friends, regain lost touch with extended family, or attempt to redefine old friendships. Madge says to Sue over coffee at work, "I'm tired of sitting here complaining about our men. Have you met any new friends or read any good books lately?" If Sue has an interest to share with Madge besides complaining, their coffee break will continue -- but in a new way.

As many men are changing, they may select the

solitude of running instead of the camaraderie of golf in order to pay attention to their feelings and body rather than rank and status. Other golfers going through Self-Discovery begin to play with a new foursome. Change is the name of the game, at this stage.

The Self-Discovery seeker asks for new responses from associates. Requests may be for honest feedback about new behavior or some candid sharing from fellow life-strugglers going through stage three themselves. Because some of their friends may choose to remain angry, the seeker's circle of friends will change to those who will share and be honest.

Children and household duties

The person in stage three sees children through new eyes. Suddenly this little person becomes an interesting teacher. Children show us how to hear grass, feel a sound, jump over cracks and sing like the rain. If we can just get our tedious business out of the way, we can take the time to really watch and listen to our feelings. Children are perpetual Self-Discoverers and wonderful teachers if adults just let them.

The reason for this new perspective is the abdication of the total responsibility for other people's behavior. When the Self-Discoverer can say to the spouse, "I'm not responsible for your feelings or behavior because you're a strong person," the same message of respect and trust carries over to children. It is now possible to see that the children will learn table manners alone if we will just get off their backs and let them imitate **our** table manners. The struggle is gone from any item where we can permit the children to learn rather than needing to teach.

The Self-Discoverer models for children how an adult takes care of him or herself. As clumsy as we often feel, children can see through our trials and appreciate the effort to learn, as they do. Seeing the adult as a learner permits children the safety of knowing they needn't have all the answers. The Self-Discoverer, while spending less time with children, usually finds that the time takes on a more personal quality.

The household duties become much less important when you are asking really important questions and finding really important answers. It's less important, for example, whether or not the dishes are done immediately after supper because you are accomplishing a more important task of talking with each other now. Besides, (1) those dishes will be there tomorrow, no matter how hard you wish they would go away, or (2) you can do the dishes before bed.

The length of time you are married helps you to get into a comfortable rut about tasks. You can either do things more automatically or permit yourself not to do them at all. So when the Self-Discoverer, who is a Mother, returns to college (a common stage 3 behavior), all tasks must be reassigned to allow Mom time to study. If the Self-Discoverer is Dad starting a new job, the whole family will need to adjust to income changes and amount-of-time spent at home. A communicating family can work out new schedules with some effort.

Children and household duties can tie down a budding Self-Discoverer. But, if he or she has a family with the willingness to help and support the new endeavor of Self-Discovery, the growth can continue. Some families are supportive because they realize that as one member of a family is freed, all members can be freed.

Communication

A person in stage 3 learns to say "I need your help. How can we work together to arrange that?", instead of saying to the family, "You never give me any time to myself," as he or she would have with stage 2 anger. It is amazing how helpful children (and even a stage 3 spouse) can be when asked for help in an honest and straight-forward fashion.

Often the Self-Discoverer will reverse his or her

communication style by saying less but with more meaning, especially if she or he previously has used talking as a screen from intimacy.

Joan was known to her friends as a talker. The men joked about her silent husband and the women loved to fill dull times with Joan's incessant but interesting chatter. When she became a Self-Discoverer, Joan talked less and softer. She decided not to be the spokeswoman for her perfectly capable husband. She began to listen and learn from her friends and associates. Nancy, however, changed from a silent and shy woman to a delightfully talkative and sharing person as she discovered that she had interesting and important things to say.

The body communication of a person in the Self-Discovery phase conveys interest, by looking at the speaker, holding the body forward with arms and legs uncrossed. The feeling is open and receptive. The Self-Discoverer is paying attention. She or he has discovered a whole new world beyond anger. The energy that had been tied up in anger is freed now for use in new ways.

The person who is learning so much self-knowledge may seem more open but this is less the case. Actually there is a strong need to pay attention to turning inward and discovering what is going on inside. With this new knowledge he or she can better communicate to interested parties. So the Self-

Discoverer may begin the process by withdrawing to consider what he or she really feels before sharing. Withdrawal and silent times fluctuate with assertion and sharing times.

Learning to communicate feelings takes a while, especially if your words fall on a spouse's angry and unresponsive ears. Many people at this stage find a confidant with whom to share struggles. The friend can provide honest feedback and a perspective about the common ties between all humans.

The Self-Discoverer learns that he or she is not a delicate flower blowing in the wind of others' opinions but a strong stalk, resilient and self-reliant. The payoff in the struggle to honestly communicate is a deep and unshakable acceptance of your newly-discovered self and confidence as you learn to relate to the important people in your world.

Work and play

The Self-Discovering person is now examining the value that work has, the amount and type of playing and the paths that he or she may travel in professional life from now on.

Work may be seen as a new adventure or a dull routine. With insight into what you really like and need, work takes on a new perspective. For example, when Mary realized that the steno pool was not her career choice and that, in fact, she hated the repetition of her tasks, she shared this with her supervisor by asking for more complicated tasks and a transfer to another department to learn new skills. To enliven her work day, Mary made a deliberate attempt to learn two new words a day and use them in conversations with her fellow employees. She even started a couple of friends on the same pastime, which drew her closer to those individuals and made her eight-hour day more interesting.

David realized that he needed outdoor work to feel good about his job, so he turned down a promotion to the "front office" to remain working with the crew. David asked himself which he needed more, the status and pay of the office job or the exercise and sunshine of his outdoor job. In making that decision, David assessed his needs according to priority so that his job took on the special quality of one selected -- not just a job.

Play takes on a whole new dimension. Very few of us permit ourselves to play -- concentrating instead on the struggle to attain status through things. The Self-Discoverer finds out what his or her style of playing is, then how much he or she needs to have fun and finds someone to share it with.

Sam had to ask himself whether he did carpentry in his spare time, making furniture and shelves, because he really liked working with wood, or because his puritan work ethic forced him to be productive even in leisure time. Sam found that the solitude, the feel of wood and the sense of accomplishment were all important to him. So he now works at carpentry when he needs those aspects in his life -- not when the laundry room needs shelves.

In stage 3, a person takes play very seriously. Play is the opposite of work so that when you work, play is an important need, not just a frivolous trivality. Giving play this credence allows you to determine what kind of play really relaxes you, leaves you with a sense of having escaped the pressure of responsibilities, and helps you focus on work at the appropriate time and with the appropriate intensity. As a nation of work-a-holics, we learned very little about recreation while growing up.

Recreation is just that, the creation, again, of focus, perspective and interest in work and life. We have all experienced the phenomena of receiving the answer to a question in the shower when we least expected it and were not even thinking about it. We need the time away that play provided. Therefore a Self-Discoverer realizes re-creation is a needed balance to work.

People possibly arrive at stage three in marriage at the same time that their normal career reassessment begins. Because of newly found needs, the seeker can change, re-evaluate or intensify a career. The exciting pioneering of opening a new business can provide the family with a task of working together rather than Dad just going to the office. In some stage 3 families, Mom's desire to return to her pre-marriage profession can change the entire focus of the family -- engendering a team spirit. Although change is sometimes difficult, it is always exciting.

Since adjustments are required by all family members, it takes a while to benefit from the "espirit de corps" of taking on a family project. Many families use this time for each member to go his or her own way with more autonomy, especially if the children are older than pre-school.

Communicating the new needs of work and play with the spouse keeps surprises from throwing the family into confusion for no reason. The Self-Discoverer is discovering that work, play and professional growth contribute to his or her life and therefore to the life of the family.

Self-concept

The self-concept of the man or woman in stage 3 is changing quickly as every day new discoveries uncover desirable and not-so-desirable facets of the personality. If the new discovery is that you have no tolerance, in fact an active dislike, for Beethoven, you may fight a "should" battle inside yourself.

A "should" battle is when your imagination shows

an internal parent-figure shaking an index finger at you saying "You should like Beethoven." But, what if you don't want to do what your parent wants? Does that make you an inadequate person? These are the conflicts of a "should" battle. "I should like Beethoven because he is a classicist, so I am inadequate (uneducated, tone deaf, inept) if I don't like Beethoven."

When the Self-Discoverer finds that he or she still is a very valuable individual whether or not he or she likes Beethoven, then an improved self-concept is gaining strong footholds. Whenever the "should" battle is won by the actual internal desire or need, the self-concept takes another step toward winning the war with the part of you that fights to make you feel inadequate.

The self-concept is now being redefined as discoveries permit the seekers to know with more accuracy what to judge about themselves. How can you know whether or not you like yourself and see yourself as positive when you don't know yourself. Every discovery provides new information giving you an opportunity to (1) like what you see and decide to keep it, or (2) dislike what you see and decide to change it, or (3) dislike what you see and decide to keep it anyway. Only after the knowledge that seeking brings can we assure ourself of a new concept.

As the Self-Discoverer progresses through stage 3 as well as subsequent stages, the self-concept becomes more and more accurate and this helps a person to gain a sense of security and fulfillment.

Techniques and tools

How to find the feelings and fears

One tool for discovering some of your feelings and fears is to complete the following 20 times: "I am ....." The blank can contain descriptive adjectives ("I am considerate"), a feeling ("I am miserable"), or status nouns ("I am a woman"). No matter what kinds of words you use, the information provided in this exercise will let you know what you think and feel about yourself. You will then be in a position to change negative images to positive images.

Linda had a vague feeling of inferiority and insecurity in public. She really wanted to be and appear as a confident, energetic person in any social circle. When she used "I am ..." sentence completion test for herself, she found that over and over the words described her fear of being seen as inadequate. "I am shy," "I am soft spoken," "I am too tall" were some of her sentences.

With the information provided, Linda began to work on speaking with more volume and clarity, looking people in the eye, standing closer to them.

She began to say to herself "I am important and worth listening to. I am confident and capable. I like myself." Slowly she began to appear as that confident, energetic person she desired to be.

With each of the negative statements, use the sentence, "Yes, that's what I am, but that's not all I am." Now that's some perspective. When we look in the mirror and see our flaws, sometimes we feel totally negative. If we own the flaw but know that "... that's not all that I am," we can keep our self-image in the perspective that permits our facing even a huge flaw.

How to change your attitude

A tool for assessing your individual situation is to fill out the following three columns on a sheet of paper.

Needs	Resources	Unmet Needs
Affection	husband	time
hugging	daughter	(80 hours a day!)
kissing		

After Helen inserted her needs, she could then ask herself, "What does this tell me? With my husband and daughter, if I need hugging and kissing, I must demonstrate affection toward them and tell them what I need. If I feel the need for 80 hours in a day, I'm usually hassled because I tried to take on more than I could comfortably handle. Maybe I could put my tasks in priority order and discard those that can wait." Taking charge always helps change your attitude.

If you have difficulty listing your resources, try to make a list of your strengths. You have many strong aspects of your personality available to you as resources to meet your own needs. What are they? Honesty? Ability to type? Ability to plan by seeing alternatives? Physical beauty? It is a strength if it provides you with a tool to meet a need. The ability to type helps a person feel secure in the fact that he or she can always get a job and support one's self. Planning ability can help a person pack more into a day if additional time is required.

By examining the information from this exercise, the Self-Discoverer can now say, "I know of some unmet needs and some of my resources. Now I can think about how to get my needs met by using those resources."

A fellow named Don discovered that he needed recognition for a job well done from a trusted person. He found that meant more to him than just recognizing his own strength. His job provided very little feedback about a job well done, only gripes when the job was not done as expected. Don's resource was his ability to relate to children. Instead of asking people at his job to meet his need for recognition, Don began to coach Little League Baseball and found the recognition from the children and their families sufficient to meet that need. Therefore, his attitude about his job and himself changed for the better.

Resources are surprisingly simple, not requiring money or education. It is easier to be positive about yourself when you realize how many strengths you already have. Each resource can be used positively even though it was a "fault" previously. A stubborn person is also a tenacious person, pursuing the goal until it is attained -- a quality ascribed to Abraham Lincoln.

An irresponsible person also can be a free-floating person -- creative and moving in new ways. A sloppy person has more important tasks to occupy his or her thinking than neatness. Each fault has a positive side. Positives and negatives are values we impose as a society. When you see the positive side of your characteristics, you realize how many resources you really have.

What a delightful surprise to realize that you have the resources to meet you own needs and can give up expecting anyone else to be responsible for them. You may elect to permit another prson to meet a need for a while, but if he or she fails you, it's all right. You can meet it yourself or find someone else who can do it.

Here are two techniques for changing your self-image:

(Set aside some time every day when you can be alone and relax in order to be able to practice these successfully, close your eyes and relax.)

1. Imagine yourself in a large mirror. (If you have difficulty at first, go look in a mirror.) See yourself **smiling.** Just relax and experience this feeling. Let it spread all through your body. (You can do this many times throughout the day with ease.)

2. Imagine yourself on a motion picture screen. Imagine that you are seeing a motion picture of yourself, acting and reacting appropriately, successfully, and ideally in some situation that you want to improve, work on, or change. Picture the scenery, the people, your actions, their actions, your reactions, their reactions, the successful results in **detail.** It is very important to picture all of this in **detail.**

Now just relax and experience these successful results for a few minutes.

(You are building a new self-image, a new way of responding to the world about you. You will find that you won't have to put out an effort to act on these areas; you will respond more or less automatically. The more often you practice them in your imagination, the more often you will find yourself responding automatically.)

Don't give up if you find it difficult to imagine yourself, others or scenery at first. Just continue on--it will still be effective -- and it will become easier and clearer with practice.

(**Psychocybernetics,** Maxwell Maltz)

A Self-Discoverer first listens to the messages from inside and then experiments with new behaviors, sometimes discovering this change is not right, sometimes it is. The new behavior can then become integrated into the personality.

When Jack decided to let himself discover new information about his spiritual self, he began by really listening to the minister in church. For a long time, Jack had found only social sanction in his church and it made him feel hypocritical to attend. He began asking himself what his spiritual needs were and then tried to find the resources for meeting them at the church. He found that his church did meet some very important spiritual needs, such as, fellowship with like-believers, a feeling of being included, and a chance to help others in service projects.

Jack also found that he needed to question his relationship with his God more than the church encouraged. To meet that need, Jack began attending classes on various theological topics at another church while also worshipping at his own church. His chief resource was his curiosity about himself and his relationship with others and his God. Thus, Jack gained a lot of comfort for his spiritual self by knowing his needs and finding ways to meet them.

When you become aware of a need, an effective tool for insuring that you will meet that need is to use the following contract. This communicates to your subconcious mind that you are serious. Having it witnessed adds impact and force to the decision.

NEED CONTRACT *

I, ________________ in realization of my need to ______________________________________

do contract to take direct and positive action on meeting my need starting on ______. In taking this action, I am aware that I have strength, power, and control of myself, thus in signing this document I recognize my responsibility to and for myself and my actions. And in the presence of a witness and on this day ____ I make a personal commitment to:

____

____

____

____

____
Signed Date

____
Witnessed Date

*Developed by Alan Schneider and Joanne Tangedahl.

Copy this form and try using it. You'll be amazed at how much help it will give you for changing your behavior.

When you are making changes, it is important to involve your heart and your head in the process. A technique to use is to ask yourself:

"What do I think about this?" and

"What do I feel about this?"

You will feel more integrated and sure of yourself if you use all of the data.

How to deal with staying in a stage by choice

The very act of choosing to stay in this stage comes from Self-Discovery, that is, knowing what you want and choosing for yourself. Here is a powerful tool to use whenever you are attempting to make a decision.

1. I want ..... I choose .....
2. I want ..... I choose not .....
3. I don't want ... I choose .....
4. I don't want ... I choose not .....

All four positions are healthy choices. The "want" portions of each option aids you in getting clear of the confusion about your desires which often clouds a decision. You decide if you want "it" or don't want "it". This does away with what other people want you to do , or what other people think you "should" do, and allows you to take responsibility for your own wants.

The "choose" portion allows you to claim your own power over the situation, take responsibility, and feel in charge. The ability to choose is a position of freedom; that is why you feel so free when you say "I choose." You are doing it by your choice, not by someone else's choice.

Check your choice to see if it is made out of **fear** or **growth**. A choice out of fear is a choice counterproductive to growth. For example, if you choose to stay in your job because you are afraid you never will get a better one, that is a fear choice. However, if you choose to stay in your job because you like your associates and you have plenty of time off to play tennis, that is a growth choice.

Considering the consequences of your choice is necessary. Sometimes we are not farsighted enough to do this and regret it later. There are always consequences inherent in any choice made.

Mike selected option 3, "I don't want to be married to my wife now because she's not fulfilling my need for sharing new ideas. However, I choose to stay married to her and get some of these needs met elsewhere." He did not want the consequences of divorce.

We may not stay in stage three forever, but most individuals who become Self-Discoverers remain that way with more or less intensity the rest of their life. This intensity will vary as the degree of comfort changes, as life situations change. Just like moving from one house to another, we move from one set of circumstances to another and adjust each step of the way by wanting and choosing depending on the situation. People are always in the process of growth so the person they were last week, or last year, is different from the person they are today. So hopefully everyone continues to be a lifelong Self-Discoverer, even though they move on to stage 4 in their marriage.

How to work with an unwilling partner

An unwilling partner is an afraid person. Predominant in the mind of the unwilling partner is the fear that an unknown life style will cause more discomfort than the current one, or maybe you, the Self-Discoverer, will leave. As the unwilling partner sees you change, he or she fears what you will find out about yourself and your feelings, specifically that you may find you do not value him or her as much as you once did. Some women even fear financial desertion especially when young children are involved.

In fairness to the unwilling partner, you need to share new discoveries with him or her in order to clear the fear of the unknown. For example, Joe says to Sally, I've discovered that I really enjoy dancing and if I go dancing with some friends because you don't want to go, it's to dance, not because I'm looking for a new wife or love you any less." Sally is a pretty strong lady, as are most people and, even if she fears what the dancing behavior will do their relationship, she can feel reassured that Joe has laid it on the line -- not lying about his whereabouts or motives.

Being candid and vulnerable to an afraid, unwilling partner is a brave and rewarding experience. The Self-Discoverer takes the chance of sharing feelings with a spouse who might lash out in fear. The payoff is the freedom from the guilt of secrecy and isolation. The book **Pairing** by Dr. George Bach cites examples of rules for communicating feelings to an intimate, that are comprehensive and clear. The goal always is to be as honest as possible.

The temptation is to protect the unwilling partner from discomfort, but this protection usually is for the speaker, not the listener, attempting to avoid conflict. However, any problem avoided lies dormant waiting to surface more destructively than ever.

If you are being honest without being hurtful, the unwilling partner can see that honesty can be beneficial. Candor can be stimulating and the communication engendered is free enough for the partner to feel reassured by being understood. Using the above example, if Joe, in an attempt to protect Sally, said "I'm going out to have some fun because you're such a party pooper and won't dance," Sally rightfully would have been hurt and attacked.

Sally has heard that (1) Joe thinks she is no fun, (2) Joe is having fun elsewhere, (3) Joe is choosing not to offer her the alternative to go, therefore, pushing her away, and (4) it is all her fault that she has two left feet. Growth that hurts that much is not attractive. An alternative explanation about Joe's new-found desire to dance added to communicating his caring for Sally would go a lot further toward helping Sally feel better and more secure with the changes.

Reassurance about future plans also is an encouragement for the partner to examine growing along with you as an alternative. Joe might say "Now Sally, this doesn't mean I'm taking three nights a week to go dancing with friends. I'd like to do so occasionally, however, knowing that you could use that time away from me to do something you like with your friends." Joe has given it his best effort. If Sally is still afraid, it is because she fears Joe is lying, or she fears Joe "accidentally" would meet another lady who would be more fun and would leave her. In either case, Joe's honesty has cleared his conscience to continue his path to Self-Discovery and has reassured Sally as much as possible without limiting himself in the process.

Here is another trap to consider. Is "moving on" a signal to leave the marriage? Is that your only alternative? Unless your Self-Discovery requires you to meditate in the Himalayas, probably not. A commitment to marriage as an institution and the partner as an individual is still possible here.

One of the many Self-Discoveries the seeker makes at this time is that the partner is a unique person, not just a mold from **Bride** magazine. What were those characteristics that made your partner attractive in the first place. Even in anger, you can, if you choose to, see positive attributes that are desirable in the partner. By using the "I want" "I choose" tool, from the preceeding pages, you may find that you want a willing partner but choose not to leave because your other needs are met specifically by your partner, or the marriage. Again, using the example, Joe could choose tennis instead of dancing to meet his needs for exercise and camaraderie, since Sally is so afraid that he will be tempted by dancing with other women.

Doug and Mary discussed Doug's fear that Mary would be so intellectually stimulated if she obtained an advanced degree, that she would see Doug as a bore. Mary itemized for Doug the many features of him and their life together that filled her needs, and thereby reassured Doug that he was still secure in his familiar place in Mary's life even though she was going on with her Self-Discovery.

Moving on always is possible. Before deciding that the end is in sight because your partner is unwilling, try being an example of enjoyable Self-Discovery to the partner, plus encouraging participation as much as possible. Some renegotiation is possible even with the most angry partner when you are willing to put out the effort.

In the last two stages "happiness" was pursued actively and was envisioned as coming from a perfect mate and a perfect relationship. The Self-Discoverer has realized that this is not so, because it is impossible. Happiness and peace come from inside. As a person develops a whole self -- mind, body, emotions and spirit -- only then is happiness truly possible. The person in stage 3 has given up the illusion that "My spouse will make me happy", and instead says, "I am happy and I want to share this." The basis for a successful relationship has formed at last.

An excellent technique for developing this stance is:

1. Assume the mental set that "I can make me happy. It is a feeling I produce. At any given moment there is enough available here and now for me to be

happy. I open myself to it."

2. Then using your five senses, begin to experience the world around you, noting what you see, hear, smell, taste and feel. Then mentally note the positive, pleasurable discoveries you make.

You will discover that your happiness level will increase easily and rapidly. You will experience a sense of power, you will feel you are truly the master of your world and not dependent on your partner to do it for you -- being left feeling helpless because at this point, your mate is unwilling to move.

How to work with a willing partner

The willing partner also is a Self-Discoverer, working at his or her own pace to grow and build the relationship. The best way to reinforce another's growth is to give him or her room to examine all the alternatives without feeling fearful that any of the alternatives would end the relationship.

Jim and Donna negotiated a deal. In order to eliminate as much fear as possible, they agreed to examine the alternative of divorce in any discussion about future change. Considering divorce is not doing it and by talking it over, Jim and Donna regularly reaffirmed their commitment to marriage and to one another ahead of other choices. When a couple faces their fears, the immobilizing stress in them is lessened.

Another reinforcement is to allow plenty of time together to share new discoveries. Turning off the TV can save many a marriage if the time is used for sharing and real communication. It is most encouraging to know that not only are you receiving benefit from Self-Discovery, but so is your partner. A bonus payoff of sharing is that each person provides new thought for the other person.

A third reinforcement is to claim your stance with not only one another, but with family and friends. "We're thinking about moving to another city." Then the partner feels supported publicly as well as privately. It always is easier with support, no matter what the change is: One of the real payoffs of being married.

Frequent checking and providing feedback helps the Self-Discoverer reflect on his or her feelings. Honest feedback includes communicating about the process of making a decision and the steps along the way -- not just the final decision.

Honest feedback and communication includes the three basic elements: (1) What we're discussing, (the topic), (2) How it makes me feel, and (3) The end result I'd like to see. For example, "When you change your mind so quickly, I feel afraid that I've had no chance to express my feelings and I'd like to have you specify the steps in between for me."

With feedback, your partner can make his or her

decision by having all the data. Your partner now has all the necessary information so he or she can respond more completely.

Honest feedback requires the Self-Discoverer to be in touch with how he or she feels about an issue in order to share it with the partner. If you can know your feelings enough to share them using the three steps, you have provided the most honest feedback available to you at the time. What more could anyone ask.

Progress in stage three is determined by the degree of Self-Discovery. If you and your partner feel that you are free individually to discover yourself and then one another, you are making definite progress. If, however, you feel limited in choices by artificially imposed limits, an internal value, ("A mother can't also be a student or her children will suffer"), then your Self-Discovery has plateaued or reached an impasse. If you can examine the limitation imposed by that value to see if you really believe it for yourself, then the Self-Discovering has begun again with new information.

Once you feel you know enough about yourself, your needs and your taste, you have sufficient data, as a couple, to refocus from your individual pursuits back to your partnership. In the next stage, Bridge Building, your needs and those of your partner, as each of you know them today, can be used to strike a workable, comfortable partnership toward the goal of remaining married.

AWARENESS
TRUST
RESPECT
RESPONSIBILITY
CHOICE
NEGOTIATION
ACCEPTANCE
COMMUNICATION

VII
BRIDGE BUILDING, STAGE 4

Identifying the stage

Up to this point in this book, we have explored stage 1, the Happiness Bubble, where the dependent connection with another person and the resulting fantasy enabled the couple to build a relationship together. The marriage was formed with the unspoken agreement that we will not go beyond this bubble. Denial, illusion, dependency, hidden anger, and fear were strong components.

Then we saw the breakdown of that fantasy which followed in stage 2, Bursting the Bubble with tremendous anger and/or depression. Oftimes, there was a complete crisis at this point in the marriage, sometimes ending in divorce, sometimes ending with a stifling resignation attempting to settle back into the illusion and not face reality. Couples who do this seem no longer to be emotionally alive. Something's wrong but it is never faced.

But if the couple's growth pattern progressed onward, next came the third stage, Self-Discovery, a very adolescent, centered on self, necessary phase, Necessary, especially if the marriage is to continue its natural evolution. With Self-Discovery the dependency ties are finally broken and the individual grows to know oneself and learns through experience that he or she has the power to meet his or her own needs.

After this long hard battle for an individual sense of self has been waged, now, we come to the fourth stage, Bridge Building. The entire marriage, its very foundation, has been tested and left shaken. If the couple managed to maintain contact during this separating process, they are probably ready to move on toward Building Bridges, connections, with each other.

Marriage now will not be a dependent, symbiotic relationship as in stage 1. No fairy Princes or Princesses here. Often heard in the fourth stage is the declaration, "This is who I am and if you don't like it, you can leave." Living up to the spouse's expectations finds no home in stage 4. Building a contact between two adults who are independent, responsible, and more whole is how they choose to continue to share their lives with one another.

Required here is an acceptance of oneself as one truly is. The knowledge gained in stage 3 is claimed as a new self-concept was born. Each person sees him or herself as an imperfect human being with both flaws and strengths. Most unrealistic expectations about oneself are now left behind.

An acceptance of the spouse as imperfect also happens when the partner took their mate off the pedestal. The trust building that will begin development in this stage is between two **real** people. Each is being responsible for him or herself, independent and yet strong enough to ask for needs to be met, making choices for oneself about this marriage and life ahead.

No longer perceived as weak and dependent, each partner is using his or her own power. In addition, they are not misdirecting energy in attempts to manipulate their spouse. They are free to choose and to ask for what they need and do not have to manipulate covertly.

There is a marked absence of parent/child type relating. She does not try to either mother him or play little girl. He is not the father authority nor is he the little boy. It is strictly an adult to adult Bridge Building phase now.

However, as an imperfect adult sometimes you feel scared, helpless and needy. You **ask** for help. This is still straight-forward, stage four adult behavior. One of the reasons to be married is to share, to love, and to be supportive to one another. The difference is that denial, illusion and manipulation are absent.

It is growth to be able to ask for your needs to be met. Growth involves risk, frightening and vulnerable. Life is risky. Accepting and adjusting to this idea aids in the forward progress of the marriage.

What has been taking place throughout the stages of this marriage so far is an adjustment process. Two different people are shifting, adjusting and figuring out how they can live together.

The power plays of the past stages were attempting to make this adjustment. Whether they were covert as in stage 1 or overt as in 2 and 3, the quarrels did not accomplish the adjustment very well. The quarrels may have been about:

-which side of the bed to sleep on
-how the kids should be disciplined
-money matters, one or two bank accounts
-who's in charge
-where should we live
-issues about friends and relatives
-sex, when, where, how, and how often
-who uses the bathroom first
-meals, what do we eat and who fixes them
-housecleaning, are we sloppy or do we have a place for everything and everything in its place
-drinking, to or not to, how much
-God and religion
-music, Country Western or classical
-what do we watch on TV
-privacy time vs. togetherness
-automobiles, what kinds, who cares for them
-what time to go to bed and get up
-where to set the thermostat

-play activities, do we do what I want or what you want, together or separate
-pets, plants, furniture
-personal hygiene or habits

Now in stage 4, it is possible to truly arrive at a satisfactory solution with these and other issues so that each of you feel like winners. In past stages, solutions were often a win-lose situation where one person won the power struggle and one lost.

Also found here in stage 4 is an acceptance of the relationship, the strongest bridge upon which to build connection. You cannot use a map to make progress on your way until you know (accept) where you are on that map. Acceptance does not mean approval. Acceptance is simply seeing what is happening in the relationship, and what is happening to you inside, at this point in time.

May says to James, "I'm not your mother. I will never quit working because it makes me feel useful. I know this is uncomfortable for you and that you want nurturing. I can nurture in other ways but I will not stop working. If you want to try it on this basis, okay. If not, I'm sorry." May is clear that she needs to take care of herself in order to have a good, solid, happy self with which to build a relationship.

The essence of stage 4 is straightforward communication, couples with a strong sense of one's identity and needs. The basis for trust and building connection with each other is now present in the marriage. The renegotiation of the marriage contract can begin now, based on new knowledge and acceptance of your self, your partner and the relationship as it is.

Sharing is possible and as Mel Krantzler expresses so well in his book, **Learning to Love Again,** "We come together in marriage to share who we are instead of what we have."

Theoretical perspectives

The Bridge Building couple comes to the relationship negotiating table with some data with which to work. Having just completed some Self-Discovery, each partner now has the data to share with a partner, thus promoting intimacy, or knowledge of one another. Erikson's model gives us two parts to consider as applicable to this stage.

First, the resolution of "intimacy vs. isolation" can be contemplated only after the self-knowledge stage of "who I am" vs. "who others think I am." Once we've decided who we are, we can offer that knowledge to another, intimacy, or withhold that knowledge from anyone, isolation. How much, and what kind of personal knowledge to share is the issue. The more we share, the more intimate, less isolated, we feel with others.

Having selected a functional place on that

continuum for ourselves, we can then move to what Erikson calls "generativity vs. stagnation." Generativity is how we choose to influence mankind, future generations, leaving one's mark on the world. our influence on future generations can show in everything from having a child, coaching little league, to writing a book or poem. If we take our self-knowledge and narrowly withhold it from the world, we stagnate. We lose the longed for contact with our fellow man: we stagnate.

A couple can choose, at this Bridge Building stage to share intimacy and grow together to influence at least their own children, but also many others. Couples usually choose to become intimate with only each other. When they see how good it feels, each begins to use the techniques and feelings to relate more intimately with world. Our generativity needs call for us to show the world how neat this is, or we stagnate.

Abraham Maslow says that an individual can now examine and meet his need for recognition and self-esteem. We need to be perceived as special, unique in the world, having special worth, to make a special contribution, to be special to someone.

The Bridge Building process is the creation of the specialness in your relationship, not like any others. This process helps us to recognize and acknowledge the specialness of ourselves and our partner. "I want to build bridges to someone special, not just anyone." So Bridge Building is the process of recognizing each one's specialness and using exactly that quality to combine to make a special relationship.

Schutz's theory illustrates the cyclic nature of our inclusion, affection and control needs. The goal for the Bridge Building couple is to gain control of the marriage so that we needn't fear that it will go away. The tools of the Bridge Building are inclusion (how much time and attention we want to spend on one another) and affection (how much and what demonstrations of caring we want to spend on each other). Each need for inclusion and affection is negotiated.

Inclusion needs include issues like (1) going out alone or together, (2) staying together at a party or not, (3) always eating meals together or not. Affection needs include issues like (1) kissing hello and goodby where and when,(2) public displays like holding hands, (3) verbal compliments, etc. The Bridge Building couple is discussing these very items to develop a functional style that meets the needs of both.

Elizabeth Kuhbler-Ross sees the next-to-the-last stage of grief as depression. Whenever we compromise, we grieve over not having it go entirely and exactly our way. We grieve over what we see ourselves giving up in the negotiation, especially before we are rewarded by the happiness of the common goal we selected with our partners.

The Bridge Building sadness comes from the difficulty of the work, also. "Why can't it be easy. Why must I work so hard, delving into risky areas, sharing scary secrets. Why can't it be easy?" The sadness is the depression before the dawn of the reward of happiness.

All of the theorists see this struggle as one of the hardest man will endure to reach the touching possible. If the rewards were not so immediate and fulfilling, the work would be almost impossible.

Sex

The possibility, in stage 4, of some very exciting and satisfying sexual encounters, comes from each being aware of the feelings present in their body, their wants, needs and desires. Each can choose to assert themselves in a free, straightforward manner to ask for what they want.

Sex is at its best between two free people who know what they want and are not playing games, attempting to use manipulative power plays on their mate. Since the dependency of the past is lessened, there can be a freer sharing. How much this enhances love-making!

Sex is one of the strongest bridges in a

relationship. Since trust is only beginning between the couple in this stage, there will be times of uncertainty and caution. When the sexual encounters contain misunderstandings and feelings of fear. The trick is to be aware of your feelings and talk them out. Then, resolution is possible resulting in another plank in the Bridge. Each conflict is a pathway to improved contact.

Exploring a new way to be together sexually and new techniques in love-making may be introduced. One partner may gather up enough courage to instigate experimental sex. A responsive partner engenders trust, thus opening the door to other new options. Some of the new behavior will be exciting and rewarding enough to keep. Some will be boring or offensive to one or both and will be discarded.

Special attention here is being given to physical touching since this can enhance and facilitate Bridge Building for most.

Very early in childhood, we were taught to restrain our natural tendency to touch others, especially those of the opposite sex. Young of most animals are born with the spontaneous expression of touching, seeking closeness, warmth and reassurance through snuggling, stroking, sucking, and enfolding. Children have been trained by adults who often feel the human body is dirty and indecent. "That's not nice." warns many parents imprinting the young, susceptible minds with the fear of physical touching and closeness.

Touching soon becomes synonymous with sex, further contributing to the prohibition. "Don't touch, sex is dirty," is heard over and over, thereby linking all touching with sexual intercourse. The closeness, warmth and nurturing that so satisfies and strengthens a couple and their relationship is thus lost. Many married couples only touch as a precursor to intercourse, rejecting all other physical closeness, fearful that it will lead to intercourse.

A couple can, however, let go of the old prohibitions carried for a lifetime beginning by realizing that physical touch does not mean sexual intercourse. Sex is not dirty anyway. Touching is rewarding and valuable in and of itself. A shift in perspective will increase the chances of a new bridge.

Effective loving touching is not manipulating another body, but loving feelings one has inside being communicated to the partner in a non-verbal physical way. The manipulative techniques often learned from reading sexual manuals, focus on the partner as an object rather than a person with whom love feelings are being shared. The partner is valued as an individual. Physical contact bridges the separateness establishing a satisfying sense of union and solidarity with one another.

When touching is not merely foreplay,

paradoxically, the sexual contact is enriched many times over. The couple is building and continually reaffirming their trust in one another, an important ingredient in any satisfying sexual relationship. A sense of security can exist, a base from which emotional well-being is experienced. The feelings of sexuality build and spontaneously flow toward the partner, back and forth, expanding the erotic arousal. The physical experience contains the spiritual and emotional components integrated from each individual's self.

Social situation

Relationships with the outside world suffer with the frustrating upheavals of stages 2 and 3. The couple will not care so much whether friends or relatives approve. Their own evaluation is now internal instead of external as in the past. The cues about how to behave together and with others come from inside now, not from social sanctions.

One partner may not so readily accept invitations from friends or relatives without checking to be sure the other feels receptive. Old unproductive friendships can leave, permitting experimenting with new and different friends plus new and different social settings.

Stage 4 couples develop relationships with single friends, gay couples, older people. After a time, some of these new relationships will fade, some will maintain. Only one partner will continue some. The important ingredient is choice. No longer locked into old patterns, there is negotiation. One did not exert power over the defeated mate.

Talking it out, making your needs known, choosing what you, individually and collectively, want is stage 4 behavior. As this negotiation proceeds, it is not always easy to build the necessary bridges to a fuller social situation.

Children and household duties

Children are often the battle ground in marriages. In stage 4, instead of accusing each other of poor parenting, each attempts to arrive at an agreeable way to parent the children. These discussions are uncertain as the new way to be together as a couple and a family is being talked out.

The children feel more secure now even with long, loud discussions. Children can tolerate a lot. They understand about working out differences because they do it all the time with their friends. They feel safer, even excited, working out new ways to live with their parents. The hope for a secure foundation once again frees children to move on with their own growth and stop worrying about Mom and Dad. Children need parents who take care of themselves and are happy to show them how it is done.

You may notice their grades improve. They may enjoy their friends more, and seem happier and more relaxed. Parents are important to children. Your improved relationship with each other comforts them profoundly.

The same negotiating process works with household duties. Never again will the wife be content to do all the "woman's work," possibly preferring instead to do the yard work or any other negotiated chore. As the talks proceed and equitable, satisfactory solutions are decided upon, trust grows: new connections are created.

Communication

Communication, although awkward in this stage, is usually on the way to improving. Most of the denial and manipulation have disappeared. Lapses into the old games don't happen very often.

The straight, leveling communication can be frightening at times, when much of the sharing is negative. Although we always feel both polarities inside -- love/hate, stay/go, like you/dislike you, want closeness/want distance, approach/avoidance, acceptance/rejection -- about any issue, often we only allow ourselves to be aware of one of the polarities, denying the other. Stage 4 couples are more aware of both sides and dare to tell each other about it. Yes, this can be frightening. After a few such encounters result in a solution compatible to both parties, the positive feeling keeps next time from feeling quite so scary. This risk is worth it.

To successfully accomplish this communicating, use more "I" messages in stage 4. "I want ... I need... I feel... I think ... I like ..." It works best coupled with listening to and really hearing the partner's "I" messages.

As self-aware and independent partners, each want to make choices, exerting their power in their own life, each is not willing to merely agree, but will voice feelings, ideas and needs. Communication becomes difficult at times. Just hang in there and keep talking it out. A solution can be found that would be acceptable to both partners most of the time.

Each success encourages further negotiation. Each person begins to feel trusting and hopeful, willing to put out effort and risk working out other areas of conflict. Communication is a vital ingredient in Building the Bridges with each other. The creation of a viable marriage proceeds in direct proportion to the willingness and ability to communicate.

Work and play

With the new data Self-Discovery provided, one or both partners may have decided that a new way is in order. Some husbands state, "I will not work such long hours any more. I want you to work and help be the breadwinner, so we can afford to buy the sailboat we've always wanted and have some fun." If she agrees, new priorities have been decided upon.

If not, they may negotiate a planned alternative like purchasing a smaller boat and saving for other vacations elsewhere. She may need more variety in travel than a sailboat can provide, so both partners can get some of what they want.

Work and play will be important areas to explore, but they will not be more important than the individual person. Before the Self-Discovery phase, identity often came from a job, especially for men. But afterwards, he realizes, "I am a person first with feelings, needs and goals. The job helps me to serve these goals." A self-directed person uses internal information to assess all areas, including work and play.

Self-concept

As stated, a stage 4 partner is more self-aware and self-directed than in any previous stage. Inner guidance is now valued, respected, followed and trusted. Trust in oneself produces self-confidence. Self-concept is stronger than ever before. A stage 4 person feels more in charge, having learned how to be assertive to ask for needs to be met.

Self-acceptance has grown with the experience of

all parts living inside of us -- strength/weakness, dependence/independence, love/hate, joy/sorrow, spiritual/animal, vulnerable/powerful. To deny the scared, needy child inside is to reject half of ourselves. We learn to love ourselves, a prerequisite to loving others.

Occasionally, the bottom drops out as some new event challenges the person, but the inner resources have been developed to rescue. Movement can go back to a positive sense of self, an acceptance of one's limitations as well as one's strengths. The building of bridges with a partner is a job requiring a stage 4 self-concept.

Techniques and tools

How to find feelings and fears

The predominant fear of losing individuality gained in stage 3 feeds the uncertainty of being able to build new connections with each other. "How can I be close again without losing myself?"
Each partner could make a list, in private, of what they want in the marriage and what they fear.

WANTS	FEARS
To be top priority to him	I'll never be
shared household duties	listened to
have sex at least twice a week	I won't be loved
save money	I'll have to always

privacy time	go along with Jim's old friends
have my own friends	Jim doesn't want sex with me
	His relatives will be more important than I am

It is amazing how much clarity there is when you write down these same thoughts that have been rumbling around in an unfocused, internal babble in your head. Now, you hold the cards for a far superior position in successful negotiation for connection.

To specifically find your fears, a technique that is used by Nathaniel Branden in **Disowned Self** is to complete the sentence beginning with "I'm afraid ..." do this 25 times. Write it, say it into a tape recorder, or best of all, do it in front of your spouse.

All of these fears must be resolved between the two of you in some satisfactory way to prevent them surfacing later to undermine your new beginnings. Fears denied and shoved away are powerful enemies to be faced later. They create such damage, when delayed, that it serves you, as a couple, to face them now. Be it a problem in the relationship, or a problem inside one of you, maybe connected to your childhood, when faced as a supportive team, friends on the same side, solution is possible. Enemies on opposing sides fight it out. Resolution requires friendship.

Harboring feelings of resentment saps your energy and prevents the Building of Bridges. A beneficial technique to help resolve your resentments involves writing down every resentment you have toward your spouse. Allow yourself a couple of hours when you'll be uninterrupted. Write everything, no matter how petty. Get every secret resentment you carry out of your system. Let yourself feel angry, sad, frustrated, confused, whatever it takes to get it all out.

Then, set the list aside. Get a drink and relax 15 minutes or so, taking a bath or something. Then go back to each resentment on the list and ask the question, "How am **I** like this?" Don't rest until you have located, within yourself, how you are similar to what you resent in your spouse. Claim this same tendency within you. Realize you have the capability to be the same way.

Benefits from this include the energy being withdrawn from the resentment, understanding your spouse **and** yourself better and zeroing in on what you need in the future to keep these resentments from happening again. All negative feelings tell you that something needs changing. Maybe you need to quit being so sensitive and learn to laugh or blow-it-off easier. Maybe you need to ask your spouse to alter his or her behavior in the future.

The successful dealing with your resentments, fear, anger and guilt -- actually all your feelings -- makes creating the kind of marriage you want a lot easier.

How to change your attitude

Our attitude did not magically come from out of the blue. It is a belief system that we have chosen. Since we designed our belief system when we were toddlers, it may not be the belief system that we want guiding our life today. Without a doubt, this system guides our life and all that happens to us.

A belief can be changed, since we were not born with it. We decided upon it and we can change it. To do this ... go through all the beliefs you hold about;

-yourself
-your spouse
-children and family
-church and spirituality
-friends and relatives
-money
-sex and closeness
-God
-work
-play

The social, emotional, physical, mental and spiritual

beliefs we hold affect all that happens in our lives. You can go through one area at a time or all together, preferably, writing them down.

As you read each belief, ask yourself:

Where did this idea originate? (Some of us have taken values from parents, church, teachers, society and never questioned their validity for us.)

Is this an idea that is important to me? (Do not try only to please others.)

Do I actually live by this or is it just empty words? (If you don't actually do it, it isn't a true value for you. Emerson says, "What you do speaks so loudly, I can't hear what you say.")

Does this belief make me and those close to me happier? (Remember, however, that immediate gratification doesn't always lead to long range happiness).

Do the consequences from having this belief turn out the way I want them? (If you believe "I'll never amount to anything," the consequences are that you won't!)

Attitude is everything. It affects every aspect of our lives. If you hold an ineffective attitude, change it. You can, now, free yourself from old unworkable beliefs.

If some of your beliefs about your spouse are blocking progress, use this technique: (1) spend some time thinking of your spouse, (2) send love to him or her, (3) see your mate surrounded and nurtured by this love. You will be surprised to find the blocks disappear after this exercise, then further Bridge Building can proceed.

How to change your behavior

During this negotiation stage 4 phase, tape record your talks with each other. Hear how you come across. Sometimes we are unaware that we are being judgmental, or realize that we just tell our side and never hear our spouse. Maybe we give unclear messages.

When a couple attempts to work out a solution to a problem, they often get stuck in blaming or will not be really clear about what's going on. Here is a problem solving model to follow.

MODEL FOR PROBLEM SOLVING

Step I: Clearly outline the problem in terms of needs.

Step II: Brainstorm all solutions (Do not evalute here).

Step III: Evaluate each solution.

Step IV: Choose one solution acceptable to **both** and decide when and how to implement the solution.

Step V: Re-evaluate to see if it's working.

Step I the step that most couples neglect. The problem is usually a conflict of needs. She may need him to be home at 5:30. He may need to feel free. They quibble for years. She feels discounted and unimportant because he won't come right home! He feels trapped or treated like a little boy being told what to do by Mommy. The problem here is **conflict about when to come home.**

Once they are clear about what the problem actually is, then they can begin to come up with solutions. Write down every idea, no matter how ridiculous. Brainstorm. Do not evaluate. Scientists use this technique because they discovered that solutions had been erroneously eliminated as useless. Scientists learned never to eliminate an idea.

Next, evaluate each solution, now eliminating those that are completely unacceptable to one or both. He will not agree to always come home exactly at 5:30 every day. She does not want to be totally in the dark about his behavior because she feels discounted. So, the solutions this couple could decide upon that are acceptable might be (1) he would call if he would be later than 6:00, (2) the arrival hour could be between 5:30 and 7:00, or (3) it could be 5:30 every day except Tuesdays and Fridays which are free times.

Next, decide upon one that is most acceptable to

both. The object is to find a solution where each of you feels comfortable, not one winner and one loser, but both winners.

After it has been tried, you need to re-evaluate. If it satisfies both parties, terrific! If not, go through the entire process again to arrive at a more feasible solution.

How to deal with staying in a stage by choice

Rarely do couples choose to stay in stage 4. When bridges are built to the partner, the pull to cross over, to experience connecion and intimacy, is powerfully inviting. We human beings require closeness, the feeling of belonging, even though we just as strongly require distance and the need for privacy.

As long as you know you are in charge of yourself, you need not fear closeness because you control moving away by your need for privacy being communicated.

But if the trust level is not strong enough to cross that bridge to intimacy as yet, here is a technique to build trust. Each partner shares one fear with their spouse, presenting that fear in detail. An atmosphere of safety and understanding prevades where two supportive friends look for a solution to fears. Remember, respect each other's feelings.

Begin with minor fears. Then choose the other fears, progressively sharing deeper and deeper fears, one at a time. The more you use this exercise, the more trust you will build. Surprise! The fear monsters you avoided are not so frightening together.

How rewarding to find someone who knows our greatest fears and is still supportive, accepting and loving. Usually we harshly reject and condemn ourselves far more often than others ever do.

Our goal with fears is to see them as manageable, to transform them to loving feelings about ourselves and others.

How to work with an unwilling partner

Partners do not grow at exactly the same rate. Growth is a web of complex factors, different for each person, yet a definable process we go through as we grow. External and internal factors both promote or retard our growth.

You are one of those external factors that either promotes or retards your partner's growth. So when you are in stage 4 and your partner is unwilling to build yet, encourage him or her by clearing up any old misunderstandings as tactfully and quickly as possible. "You may still think I resent your playing poker on Friday nights. I really don't anymore. I enjoy the regular evening of privacy." Your spouse is not a mind reader. He or she can only work on information from the past unless you update.

After the Self-Discovery stage, you now realize that you are responsible for making yourself happy or sad. If, in the past, you became angry and created a scene whenever your partner went out, he or she may believe you still feel resentful. Reluctant to ever bring up the subject again, it becomes a barrier, interferring with Bridge Building.

Communicate what you **now** believe, so that your partner can be more willing in the future. Engender hope by being your new honest, vulnerable self. If you are happy, show it! When we feel really good, we seldom voice our appreciation. Because pain demands change and pleasure does not, it pushes us to fuss in hope of change.

We need some positive reinforcement here. Tell your partner what you like -- we all need positive strokes. Make a top priority of words like "I like ..." or "I appreciate ..." Complaining won't help the unwilling spouse become a willing one.

You soon realize how impossible it is to move on to stage 5, Reconnection, without your partner. Who can connect if you don't have someone willing to connect with you? Another tool is to work on the imagination level, a powerful generator of movement.

Spend some time each day imagining your marriage with your mate as you want it to be. Picture it, feel it, think about it. You are programming the future direction your marriage will take.

A man now in a good job, imagined one day he would be supervisor and make more money. He saw himself getting a bigger paycheck, going on a vacation to the Bahamas, giving orders to others at work. He visualized the future. He saw the possibility. We dare to dream when we believe it's possible.

How to work with a willing partner

Just as it is easier to carry a heavy load with help, it is easier to make progress when you have a partner who will help. Say, "Thanks for the help, partner. I appreciate that." The oftener you say it, the more power it has.

Also, tell your spouse what you want, not only what you don't want. When parents communicated to us as children, something wrong was pointed out loud and clear. Yet, little people are seldom told how to please their parents. So when parents fuss, kids change to something else. Often, that isn't right either so they end up feeling frustrated in their efforts to please. We don't know what **to do** -- we only know what **not to do.**

"Hold me close awhile when we first go to bed and talk to me a little bit about how you feel about us. This makes me feel safer and closer to you and then I'm more receptive to sex."

Or, "I liked dinner so much tonight because we sat and talked awhile at the table. You told me how you felt about work and I loved it when you reached out and took my hand. I felt loved and close to you."

Building trust is of paramount importance. When your mate shares fears, be supportive. Create a safe atmosphere so that future Bridge Building communication can take place.

Judgment or criticism needs to be left behind. Evaluate whether things are working, not if they're right or wrong. Build an attitude of acceptance. That is not approval of everything, or sacrifice of your needs.

It is trust in each other that change can happen, where love is involved in the process. When there's acceptance, there's accurate, uncritical feedback.

Feedback is a way of giving help: it is a corrective device which helps a person learn how well behavior matches the intended message.

Here are some useful points to remember about feedback:

(1) Be specific rather than general. Talk about what's happening now between you. Tell your partner how his or her behavior is affecting you.

(2) The needs of both of you are taken into account. If you give feedback without taking the needs of your partner into consideration,

or taking your needs into consideration, one of you will be injured.

(3) Leave criticizing, forever. Instead, describe your reactions and feelings to your partner. Use "I" messages.

(4) Talk about only those issues that can be affected. Don't give feedback about your husband's loss of hair. How would he change that?

(5) Consider when you choose to give feedback. Don't do it; (a) in front of friends, (b) when you or your mate is tired, (c) just when you're leaving for a party, or (d) when there is some other trauma going on in the relationship. We hear feedback a whole lot easier when it is well-timed.

(6) Always check for corrections. Sometimes our feedback is based on an error in perception.

A final thought about feedback: Help not asked for is seldom perceived as help. So set up some structured time for feedback, possibly an hour after dinner every Thursday, designated as "feedback time." Then save your feedback and refrain from jumping right in and telling your mate what needs changing. Feedback is important but use some finesse.

When you want to evaluate your progress in this

stage, feedback and good communication techniques are essential. The focus is on trust, communication and negotiation. So when you are each alone, (1) evaluate by yourself how you are progressing in each of these three areas. Give it a percentage rank, such as, 90% for trust, 80% communication and 60% negotiating. (2) List the factors you believe are blocks. (3) List what needs to be done to insure progress. Then (4) meet together and discuss it with the goal in mind of moving on to stage 5.

VIII
RECONNECTION, STAGE 5

Identifying the stage

Reconnection is the touching of two separate people in a touching filled with so much trust that it feels supremely safe.

Reconnection is a knowledge about oneself, in relation to the other person, that is comfortable and secure.

Reconnection is an overwhelming sense of trust in oneself that no matter what the partner says or does, "I know, down to my toes, that I am a whole self, able to handle anything without being destroyed."

Reconnection is a floating level of comfort in the daily decision-making process that lets one say, "If he is not comfortable about this situation, I can trust him to tell me so we can alter it."

Reconnection does not come about as a plan. It is more like waking up and finding yourself there. Reconnection is walking away from a discussion feeling like a winner, loved and considered. The ingredient most sought is that both feel like winners.

Reconnection is two independent, self-knowledgeable, responsible people, who have enough trust and acceptance, choosing to create together their own unique relationship that has an atmosphere for growth, supportive sharing, and a spiritual, emotional bonding. It is a place of love.

Many marriage rules say that if you will just do these things, you will have a happy marriage. If you will just:

(1) give more than your 50%

(2) make love every night

(3) kiss and make up often

(4) don't let the sun go down on your anger

(5) be considerate about the partner's needs,

then your marriage is sure to succeed. When your partner does not follow these rules to your expectations, you immediately assume that "She doesn't love me or she'd follow the rules and do all these things."

Let's look at another perspective on the platitudes offered above. The rules are not guidelines to follow to get you there. The rules are a description of what it is like when you arrive. When you feel secure, connected,

(1) you automatically give more than 50% because it takes nothing away from you. It requires no sacrifice of your needs.

(2) you automatically make love every day because making love becomes a redefined act of two whole people sharing intimacy. Intercourse is only one part of making love. Touching hands at the right moment, can

show more intimacy than you believed could exist.

(3) you automatically kiss and make up often because you are not feeling distanced, pushed away, by your behavior. You can feel secure in your worth and your partner's love, no matter how afraid he or she acts.

(4) you automatically stop the sun from going down on your anger because your anger is not the anger that festers and smoulders underneath. Your anger can come out at the appropriate times and in the appropriate amounts in proportion to the situation. In addition, your anger is not a signal of the relationship's end, but a signal of an issue to deal with, successfully, as you have many others.

(5) you automatically are considerate of the other person's needs. That is easy to do when you meet another's needs without expense to the meeting of your own. You can only do this when you know your own needs.

When you have made Reconnection, you trust. Many a disillusioned spouse has said, "If I only could find someone I could trust, then I could be happy." The trust that is sought, however, is not in a partner, but in yourself.

When you can trust yourself to not only live through but benefit from **any** response your partner could give, then you can risk saying and sharing anything. "This really is a human being, just like me, with fears just like mine." The trust is so complete that if the partner could read your mind, it would still be safe. Wow!

"Why is this RE-connection then? I've never been that open to anyone, not even my beloved." When you are in the Happiness Bubble, you trust your partner, until he or she has failed to come through for you, thereby moving you to stage 2, where the Bubble Bursts. Most of us trust others until our trust is betrayed, i.e. we feel hurt.

The RE-connection is the re-establishing of that almost naive trust with the one major difference -- that now the trust is in yourself. There is no need to deny aspects of the partner or decrease the worth of yourself or your mate, as a person.

For an individual to grow to a place where connection is possible, much sorting out of beliefs and values has taken place. One wife said, "I used to think that what my Mom said about marriage was the ultimate, so I tried to make my marriage one my Mom would approve of. Now I see that the way Mom was married was not for me, it was for her. I had to find my own way."

If we let "Father Knows Best" or any portrayed

marriage tell us what to have in our marriage, we deny our own individuality, our specialness. The most magic and powerful ingredients in the marriage are the two special, unique people who make it up. The marriage is special in direct proportion to the feeling of specialness each partner has for themselves, and for the other. Each person is here by choice. Inside, a stage 5 person may say, "I don't need to be with you to survive or be happy, but I want to. I like the way I feel being married to you better than I feel being alone."

The Reconnected marriage may look intriguing. The feelings one receives in the presence of a Reconnected couple are powerful and curious. One wonders what that couple has going for them. It does not look like any other marriage in the world. Two creative people have designed, hammered and constructed a viable, functional and comfortable relationship that will be unique.

Theoretical perspectives

Erik Erikson is one of the few theorist who has divided adulthood into stages, whereas Freud labeled anything after adolescence as Adult, assuming that growth stopped there.

The Reconnected couple is struggling for a resolution of what Erikson calls "integrity vs. despair." Integrity is an integrated approach to life, integrating common values into the roles of parenting, partnering, working, socializing. An integrated individual knows his beliefs and interweaves them into all facets of his life, consistently, easily and joyously. An integrated couple relationship forms a life based on those beliefs and values that are common, shared.

For instance, an integrated individual may have a belief that honesty is always a priority. Now, to tell a little white lie to the kids would be the same degree of violation as to lie on the IRS 1040 or to lie to a friend. If honesty is always important, it is important in everything.

Now, an integrated couple, let's say, has the same value. it would be a violation, then, to tell a little white lie about having other plans to get out of a social engagement, as much of a violation as lying to the partner. So values and beliefs are interwoven into all aspects of a partner's relating and all aspects of the couple's relating.

The opposite of this integrity for the person or couple is despair. Despair is hopelessness: "We'll never make it. It's out of control." If the pieces do not connect to form a whole, it is hopeless and confusing and alone. We have all felt moments of despair, when all of our beliefs and values seem incapable of providing us with peace. We sort through and re-examine, until we make a new way of fitting the pieces together to form an integrated whole.

Abraham Maslow says that in the order of needs, the one we can attend to last, after all others are met is Self-Actualization. He describes these Self-Actualization needs as those that maximize a person's potential. These needs are not necessary for life functioning, Maslow says, but are the luxury of allowing yourself to do something just because it is fun or beautiful or exciting.

The couple formed by two Self-Actualized people selects a style of living and learning that broadens the person's horizons, expands his choices. In this stage, people begin to paint, write poetry, till the earth, seek universal meaning and abstract truth. It is obvious why this need is placed after all the others. In order to spend the time and energy expanding, one cannot be worried about how to pay the bills or get kids to ballet or baseball practice.

The meeting of these needs is private and quiet. Some people call them "deep", profound needs.

Schutz describes the Reconnected relationship in terms of its need for control. The Reconnected couple has tried every known method of controlling themselves, each other and their world. The bottom line for such an effort is that the only control there actually is comes from giving up the kind of control we were taught would solve our feelings of helplessness. That was control of others. The most productive use of control, then, becomes controlling one's own fears so that they do not block the natural control imposed by growth.

The one controlling factor in a Reconnected couples' life is change; people and things, changing and moving. Control of that irrevocable fact comes from letting it happen, letting life and each other change as growth determines. That is the only control we have ever had anyway, no matter how many ulcers we received from trying.

Elizabeth Kuhbler-Ross describes the last stage of grief as acceptance. We have grieved over the loss of magical dreams and awakened to the acceptance that reality, humanness and life are better than any old dreams. Now, we can go on, enjoying what we have, leaving behind the attempts to impose rules on an already neat life.

The key to a Reconnected couple's growth is that it is not over. Now, it can begin. Learning and loving can be pure and unhampered by the despair, depression, stagnation of the previous fears.

Sex

The Reconnected couple finds sex to have two new facets. The first is anything goes that is loving to yourself and your partner. "I don't need to fear rejection for offering a new idea, or being sleepy, because I'm secure in the love, respect and acceptance of my partner."

The second facet is that sex is more than intercourse, for more places than the bedroom. A Reconnected couple can make love with their eyes across a crowded room. A brief touch or loving word can excite the partner to flush with pleasure. The intimate knowledge they share with each other is emotionally, spiritually and physically naked.

The emphasis on sex, as a Reconnected couple, is on intimacy, the feeling of oneness achieved. In previous stages, emphasis could have been on the number of times you have intercourse in a week, the amount of time in foreplay, the number and initiation of new activities, but **not** the feeling.

Sex for a Reconnected couple is straight forward, lacking the angry games of previous stages. The bedroom activities can be beautiful and trusting, even if you have a current difference. Sex is not withheld in anger or flaunted in jealousy. Those are past methods of handling.

The Reconnected couple is usually sexually faithful, not because of a promise or rule, but because of a trust level unable to be achieved elsewhere. "I don't have time to develop another relationship to the point of sex. I'm too busy enjoying the one I've got." It requires commitment and attention to maintain the Reconnected level of intimacy. With this much beauty in a relationship, sport sex looses it's plastic lustre.

Since so much sexual expression is felt in words or thoughts, there is less urgency in making physical love as a sign of love. When making love takes place, it is just that ... making love, unconditional, accepting and secure. If the techniques do not work right, that's OK. There is always another time.

Social Situation

Since creativity is the key aspect of Reconnection, the couple can design social situations to meet the needs of each member. One husband and wife spent fun evenings together sewing the Christmas gifts the family gave. Another couple threw a painting party to repaint their living room. Another had a vegetable party and invited two other families to put up vegetables for the freezer. The Reconnected couple can design a group activity that meets several needs and also relinquishes many role boundaries. The women paint: the men slice vegetables.

The Reconnected couple needs concentrated couple-time in which to share and discuss their life and growth. If life gets too hectic for a quiet evening of talking, a Reconnected couple partner begins to feel adrift, unplugged from the vitality of the connection. The time spent in intense sharing is not usually long, but must be private and safe.

The Reconnected couple partners are best friends. Each gives the other the space and respect accorded a best friend. Thus, in any social situation that joy comes from being together, doing almost anything that permits creative learning and fun.

Children and household duties

Couples moving to stage 5 and feeling reconnected greatly appreciate children as people, human beings with human needs. The partners each see some "little child" in themselves and the other that is valuable.

Usually, Reconnected couples have older children because they began bearing their children in stages 1 and 2. In fact, many Reconnected couples have only each other after the children are gone from the nest.

Because the Reconnected couple has an open awareness to each other's needs, the household duties and child care duties are usually discussed and distributed according to the family design. For instance, one couple shared all duties equally and shared all money earning duties equally. The husband and wife both worked full time and came home to immediately do household and child care tasks until it was finished so they could relax.

Another couple budgeted a housecleaning person to help save them time to relax together. Then, they shared the balance of tasks. Another couple decided that he would work full time for the five years it took to bear whatever children they would have, then she would work to give him some time off to spend with the children. Another couple spent Saturday mornings cooking dinners for the freezer so that dinner times could be more relaxed.

Notice, no couple is exactly alike. The Reconnected couple designs their own plan and redesigns it when it fails to meet the family's needs. As long as meeting needs is the priority, any plan designed to meet needs works.

Children receive the message from the Reconnected couple that (1) paying attention to individual needs is important, (2) they are creative enough to come up with a solution that will work to satisfy all, and (3) they are part of a team whose task is to function together as happily and smoothly as possible and (4) that being a responsible adult can be fun and attractive.

If you can teach your children how much fun it can be to be responsible and responsive, they will have, at their command, a tool for making their own happy style. What parent doesn't want for his child to be happy? You are, in effect, teaching your child not what to choose, but how to choose.

Communication

The Reconnected couple has communication at

many levels; verbally, mentally, facially, behaviorally. The verbal communication contains "I" messages not "You" messages of the previous stages. Instead of "You didn't take out the garbage", the Reconnected couple can say "I need you to carry out the garbage for me, please."

The mental communication is a unique kind of understanding that comes from trust, knowledge and time spent together. A husband can know his wife so well that he can "feel" her tense up when someone makes a crude joke. A wife can know her husband so well that she "knows" how he will feel in response to an inquiry from a child or a request to go to the store. This is far different from the guessing and assumptions of the Happiness Bubble.

The facial communication comes from concentrated watching, a deep knowledge from being together over time. A wrinkled brow gives a non-verbal message, a twinkling eye gives another message. You know because you checked it out. Besides your partner promised to let you know if it changed. The Reconnected couple reads these signals pretty well, especially in the times of quick decisions, and that keeps functioning smoother.

When Mary and John were asked to a party by friends, John noticed Mary's eyes wrinkle for just a second. He responded that he and Mary would discuss it and let them know. At home, Mary said,

"Thanks for not accepting that invitation. I really wanted to spend that evening with my folks." John said, "I thought so. Your eyes wrinkled in your way of seeming worried about something."

The most obvious absence in the Reconnected couple's communication is blaming. No blaming. Imagine being in a relationship with another person where no one ever said anything was your fault. No one judged you as bad or inadequate in any area. Can you imagine being comfortable enough to say, "I did that, and its seems dumb now." It is a lot easier to correct yourself for a mistake if you know your spouse won't say it first.

Self-concept

Each member of the Reconnected partnership has examined him or herself with questions like, "What do I believe about myself as a person? How worthy do I think I am? What is it about me that makes me special?" The Self-Discovery phase of marriage is like the growing up of two adolescents. The Reconnected stage of marriage is the touching of two mature adults.

An emotional adolescent does not have the capacity to experience a Reconnected marriage. As the adolescent develops a self-concept, then a maturity of opinion about one's self permits connection to another grown person.

The partner in a Reconnected marriage values him or herself highly enough to say "I deserve to be happy and comfortable and have my needs met. Further I am creative enough to design a way to get this without hurting anyone."

It is falsely labeled "conceit" when a person says "I deserve to have my needs met." Some of our most basic needs, as humans are (1) to be helpful, (2) to be appreciated (3) to help others. "I'm getting a need met, when I meet my need to help others, by helping you." Read that again, and out loud!

You have a need, as a human, to help, to give, to bestow love, to comfort. When you get your needs met, the world is a better place for everyone, both the receiver and the giver. You know you are there when you cannot tell the difference between the giving and the receiving.

Techniques and tools

How to find the feelings and fears

The most recurrent problem in a Reconnected marriage is to learn the vocabulary of feelings and fears. The trust you have developed with your partner lets you want, even yearn to share your feelings, but you don't always know how to label it.

You want it to (1) be accurate in meaning, (2) claim the responsibility so as not to blame or criticize and (3) honestly reflect your desired response. "I get scared when I don't know the balance in the checking account. I need to know that I'm not overspending when I write a check. That's why I'm asking for the balance all the time."

The problems in designing such a message are incredible. You have to know that the uneasy feeling at the check-out counter this morning was because he hadn't recorded the balance in your checkbook, again. You have to be able to label that feeling as scared, then ask yourself what you are scared of.

You imagine what could happen if you had no money there and you wrote this check. You'd be overspent and that you don't want. You also have to be able to say "I need you to record the balance in the checkbook," instead of "You're a jerk for not recording the balance like I asked you to."

A list of feeling words follows. It will help your labeling process to have used each word in a sentence. One couple, who was learning, took the list on an auto trip and used them while driving on the vacation. They communicated feelings by labeling behavior.

"I feel disappointed when I'm kept waiting for someone."

"I feel excited when we discuss a trip."

"I feel __________ when __________ ."

LIST OF FEELINGS THAT PERSONS HAVE BUT OFTEN FAIL TO IDENTIFY

Abandoned
Adequate
Adamant
Affectionate
Agony
Almighty
Ambivalent
Angry
Annoyed
Anxious
Apathetic
Astounded
Awed

Bad
Beautify
Betrayed
Bitter
Blissful
Bold
Bored
Brave
Burdened
Calm
Capable
Captivated
Challenged
Charmed
Cheated
Cheerful
Childish
Clever
Combative
Competitive
Condemned
Confused
Conspicuous
Contented
Contrite
Cruel
Crushed
Culpable

Deceitful
Defeated
Delighted
Desirous
Despair
Destructive
Determined
Different
Diffident
Diminished
Discontented
Distracted
Distraught
Disturbed
Dominated
Divided
Dubious

Eager
Ecstatic
Electrified
Empty
Enchanted
Energetic
Enervated
Enjoy
Envious
Excited
Evil
Exasperated
Exhausted

Fascinated
Fawning
Fearful
Flustered
Foolish
Frantic
Frustrated
Frightened
Free
Full
Fury

Gay
Glad
Good
Gratified
Greedy
Grief
Groovy
Guilty
Gullable

Happy
Hate
Heavenly
Helpful
Helpless
High
Homesick
Honored
Horrible
Hurt
Hysterical

Ignored
Immortal
Imposed upon
Impressed
Infatuated
Infuriated
Inspired
Intimidated
Isolated

Jealousy
Joyous
Jumpy

Kicky
Kind
Keen

Laconic
Lazy
Lecherous
Left out
Licentious
Lonely
Longing
Loving (love)
Low
Lustful

Mad
Maudlin

Mean
Melancholy
Miserable
Mystical

Naughty
Nervous
Nice
Nutty

Obnoxious
Obsessed
Odd
Opposed
Outraged
Overwhelmed

Pain
Panicked
Parsimonious
Peaceful
Persecuted
Petrified
Pity
Pleasant
Pleased
Precarious
Pressured
Pretty
Prim
Prissy
Proud

Quarrelsome
Queer

Rage
Rapture
Refreshed
Rejected
Relaxed
Relieved
Remorse
Restless
Reverent
Rewarded
Righteous

Sad
Sated
Satisfied
Scared
Screwed up
Servile
Settled
Sexy
Shocked
Silly
Skeptical
Sneaky
Solemn
Sorrowful
Spiteful
Startled
Stingy
Stranged
Stuffed
Stupid
Stunned
Stupefied
Suffering
Sure
Sympathetic

Talkative
Tempted
Tenacious
Tenuous
Tense
Tentative
Terrible
Terrified
Threatened
Tired
Thwarted
Trapped
Troubled

Ugly
Uneasy
Unsettled

Violet
Vehement
Vital/Vitality
Vulnerable
Vivacious

Wicked
Wonderful
Weepy
Worry (Worried)

Zanie

Another tool for stage 5 functioning is to try to imagine exactly how you would like any given situation to turn out. For example, in deciding how to entertain a couple of friends, your spouse wants to take your friends out to dinner, and you want to cook and have a quiet meal at home. You want the intimacy of home, the saving of money, the access to telephone or children, and the freedom from the out-to-dinner entertainment cycle. As you imagine the possible outcomes, you have more data with which to decide what to actually do. If you know what you want, IN TERMS OF FEELINGS, you can get the needs met in a number of creative ways. You could;

1. hire a sitter to take the kids elsewhere and cook at home.
2. find an intimate but inexpensive restaurant.
3. have some intimacy by sharing as you dress and prepare for the evening.
4. etc.

The most important word in that list is "ETC". If you know what would make you FEEL good in the situation, you can come up with many creative ways to meet your needs.

How to change your attitude

Each issue of daily functioning is put through a stage 5 attitude filter. Where you used to feel compelled to insist on your way, now you can see the partner's behavior, not as a challenge, but as an offering, to work it out.

When we feel controlled, challenged, afraid and powerless, we lose our powers to negotiate for our needs, even to perceive the situation with any accuracy. The Nazi Germans used this technique of surprise and fear to terrorize a nation. However, when we feel confidence in our power to meet our need to feel comfortable and secure, we need not fear. We can then negotiate with gracious feeling toward a partner.

Once you have experienced any Reconnected feeling, it is worth all the work to recapture, regarding even the most sensitive issues. If you are perceiving your partner as attacking you, therefore feeling that you need to defend yourself, you can change that attitude by focusing on your partner not as an enemy, but as a partner against the common enemy of stress, tension and misunderstanding.

If you are perceiving your world as lacking for you, as having scant supplies to meet your needs, you can refocus to see the resources that ARE available to you. For example, if your job is providing no positive feedback or recognition, you are perceiving a lack of those reassurances for you. What resources do you have to;

(1) get some feedback on your job
(2) get some recognition in another area of your life.
(3) see the lack of recognition as a learning experience.
(4) get another job.

As you focus on these resources, many others begin to occur to you. You will find your attitudes literally transforming. You, in your infinite creativity, design the path to get the right feeling. It will take work. It is not easy. You were provided with all the capability and equipment to do the job.

If you can see your partner as just that, a partner, and your world as manageable, you are reconnected to your partner and yourself.

How to change your behavior

How does a Reconnected couple behave? Do they ever fight, exchange harsh words, throw a dishtowel? Sure. We're all just people! But feelings come out at more appropriate times and in more appropriate amounts. In addition, when a feeling comes out, no matter what feeling, it is OK. You are entitled to feel everything you feel. Everyone has a spell of feeling down now and then, even stage 5 couples, and they might communicate like this:

"I can't take another minute of your screaming, Billy."

"Honey, he just wants supper!"

"I need some space. Will you both help me by going to the other room so I can finish preparing supper?"

-- as compared to --

"You're a bad child for screaming like that. Get out of here!"

"What kind of a mother are you, kicking a hungry kid out of the kitchen?"

"Who needs your help? Get out of here, both of you, before you make me go crazy!"

In the two above exchanges, the feelings are the same. The messages are entirely different. The first contains no labels of judgment or criticism. It just says the need and asks for cooperation -- stage 5 communication. The second message sounds like an attack because the speaker assumes no responsibility for his or her feeling. "It's all their fault." How could you ever expect cooperation by blaming? It seldom works.

The behavior of communicating clearly and responsibly, of treating yourself with respect and courtesy, of acting secure and in charge all show that you are connected to your personal power source.

The behavior of sharing tasks, concerns, feelings and responsibilities all reflect a Reconnected couple's functioning. Even a task as difficult to accomplish as a move of your home or a job change can run fairly smoothly without blaming and criticism, giving the partner credit for doing the best he or she can. The behavior of Reconnected partners flows because there is trust, freedom, choice, responsibility, cooperation and caring.

How to deal with staying in a stage by choice

The choice of staying in a mode of connection

with your partner requires lots of work. Every issue of importance will go through the process of:

HE

→1. How do I feel?
2. What do I need?
3. What do I want?
4. How far am I willing to go?
└5. How do I feel now that I've changed?

SHE

→1. How do I feel?
2. What do I need?
3. What do I want?
4. How far am I willing to go?
└5. How do I feel now that I've changed?

The arrow illustrates the movement back to question 1, as often as necessary.

Staying Reconnected requires a regular update on what each has learned about him or herself and renegotiation about where it fits in the functioning of the relationship. As one gets used to being Reconnected, the comunication becomes more practiced, more automatic, not only the communication with each other but the questions you ask yourself.

Don't you get bored being smooth so much of the time, never fighting or struggling? How can it be boring to get to really know yourself and your partner and the relationship? If you get bored and feel stifled, you have stopped growing. If you will be yourself, float along, growth will naturally happen. Growth is the natural state of living things. Keeping tabs on growth is a full time job.

But isn't the work tiring and sometimes frustrating? Yes! and yes! Doing the hard work of removing the blocks that inhibit growth, relating and communicating can bring sweat to the brow, tears to the eyes and even stiffness to the neck. You will never work harder and never be paid in more valuable coin. If it stops being worth it, go back to stage 3 and rediscover the unmet need that is surfacing for you.

How to work with an unwilling partner

Being in the Reconnected stage with an unwilling partner is like being a plug with no electrical outlet. There's no juice ! No current! It takes two to connect, two who are willing, because the connection is so powerful.

One of the fundamental facets of home electrical current is that it is alternating, not always flowing in the same path or with the same force. Thus, a Reconnected relationship has a fluctuating energy flow, but the light stays on in spite of the variations.

Once a connection is made, it can be assumed that a need is met on both sides and now is fixed and finished. Now **that** would be boring. Part of Reconnection is changing your mind, your feelings, your behavior. In fact, a built in checking system with each other could keep you informed of the changes as they appear.

"I thought you enjoyed our regular fun night with Bob and Nancy. Have you changed your mind about our evenings?" "Well, I'm feeling stifled because it's too regular. I like Bob and Nancy and I want to enjoy other friends as well. Is it all right with you if we make it alternate weeks?" "Sure, as long as I know where you stand."

Once you have (1) discovered a feeling, (2) labeled that feeling and the attendent need, (3) discussed how to get the need met, (4) selected an alternative to try, THEN (5) set a time limit on trying the new alternative and (6) re-evaluate your decision. Then the partner who seemed unwilling can feel that he or she has regular control of the selections and recapture the willingness.

Could it happen that you discover that you don't want to be married any more? Of course it could. Faced head on, this issue can even feel positive. People who know and trust one another can decide that their individual paths must supercede their common path.

The worst that could happen is to have discovered

who you are and then, further discover that you need to move on. Remember some very important things.

First, you can go your way with much more knowledge than you have ever had before, about your needs, likes, feelings and self in general. Second, you come out knowing that you gave to the relationship all you had to give. You need not feel guilty for things not done or said. Third, you end up with the knowledge of having formed a successful relationship, at least once in your life. Now you know how to do it again, when the time is right.

There is sadness when you decide that one part of your life is over, kind of like moving from the family homestead. The expectation that a lifetime decision to stay married is almost always a devastating idea to give up. It always intrigued me that people could promise how they would feel in ten years when needs and life would be so different.

If you can promise to allow and encourage your mate to grow in your presence, that's all there is. Then you are married to a person, growing, alive, exciting, different every day.

How to work with a willing partner

A couple of sentences that sound good, no matter how the day shapes up are "I choose to be married to you one more day," and "I like being married to you." Another is "I know you're doing the very best you can. You can handle it." Anyone would like to hear any of those sentences every day. They wouldn't even be bored if they heard them often.

When you are reassured by your partner, especially without asking for it, that it will all work out, and that he or she has confidence in you, even the stormiest weather looks sunny. Reassurance that your partner still cares, trusts and loves you is our most frequent need.

Another sure way to reinforce each other is to play "Remember when ..." Reminisce about the days (even those just a month ago) when you were unable to discuss a certain issue, or when you felt particularly persecuted. A concrete way to share accurate perceptions is to keep a feeling diary. Make a notation, every day, of one sentence describing your feeling for the day. If you care to elaborate, that's fine. One sentence is sufficient. Then, when playing "Remember when ..." bring out your feeling diary and read selected passages. It will show you how far you have come.

If, in using the communication techniques in this book, you still feel in doubt about your partner's perceptions, listen to your own feelings. "How do I feel in the relationship now?" The first sharing of this kind might go like this: "I'm afraid to get used to this comfort for fear it will go away," or "I find myself guessing about what you're feeling these days.

Would you be willing to share with me?" or "I'll share what I see going on if you will do the same."

If ever you doubt your partner's need for feedback, ask. "Do you get tired of hearing me say these things?" You may get a response such as "I feel nagged," or "You can tell me that a thousand times a day." That one usually follows a reassurance. Most of us need lots of reassurance, especially from those close to us.

The one thing honest feedback is NOT is an analysis of your partner's feelings and motivations. It is a personal intrusion to project your opinions on your partner. Sentences like "You're just tied to your mother's apron strings" are accusatory and do not provide any workable information.

To evaluate the state of your relationship, a progress report can be recorded on your calendar. Pick a symbol, like * for a happy day. Pick another symbol, like XX for a sad, mad, disappointed, hassled day. If you are in doubt, record the one that seemed to dominate the day. Now, at the end of the week, if you have more XX's than *'s, there is something you are worried about, afraid of, nervous about. Find out what it is. Discuss it with your partner and enlist help.

"I'm feeling jumpy these days. How do I seem to you? Could you help me pinpoint when it began and what might be behind it?" Your goal is the vast majority of * days.

Often when we have mostly XX days, we accuse events of teaming up to attack us. When each partner feels safe from attack, neither feeling attacked nor feeling the need to attack, then you are progressing. When each partner feels comfortable from judgment and criticism, neither judging nor being judged and criticized, then you are progressing. When this safe and comfortable feeling prevades and dominates each day, you are progressing toward the goal of having plenty of * days -- an admirable goal.

As this chapter on stage 5 draws to conclusion, it is important to remember this is not the end. It is the beginning of creating that unique relationship that is especially for the two of you -- created by the two of you.

The relationship will need to be constantly nurtured or it will not flourish. If you had a beautiful plant, you would never let it go unwatered or without sunlight: it would die. Never let your relationship go uncared for or, yes, it will die.

Also, a constant cycling back through stages 3,4, and 5 again will handle each new issue as it comes up. Just realize that when something big, such as the kids all leaving home, happens, both of you will need to evaluate alone "Who am I now that the duties of being a parent have changed?" (stage 3). Then there is "How will we be together now?" (stage 4) and then comes stage 5, Reconnection in a new and different way.

This gives excitement, growth and new life to your relationship. What a way to be together!

IX
PARADOXES

Life is a constant encounter with paradoxes. "This just doesn't make any sense," is the cry when encountering one. The type of mind that relies heavily on the logical and analytical thinking, feels confused.

Since relationships do not escape this confusing dilemma of paradoxes, an entire chapter has been devoted to some paradoxes operative in marriage.

Webster defines paradox as "a statement that is seemingly contradictory or opposed to common sense and yet is perhaps true, a tenet contrary to received opinion." People unknowingly eliminate the valuable information available by rejecting paradoxes immediately.

Paradox in action is found in the natural growth process, the constant interplay between closeness and distance, between separation and connection. Recall the Walt Disney time-lapsed photographs of blooming flowers. The definite rhythm to this unfolding, surging forth alternating with seeming non-movement, an ebb and flow, is the growth process of all of life including relationships.

Connection-separation evident in the stages of marriage, show that stage 1 contains a definite connection. The fantasy and dreams involved are necessary to make the bonding between the two. The onset of stage 2 finds a pulling away, a distancing, a separation as the dream bubble bursts. Then, we see complete pulling away with stage 3, where the twosome divides, each to gain a separate sense of self, similar to the growth that comes with the division of cells.

Two separate adult selves who can now come together to relate, to work as a team, see the beginning aspects of connection in stage 4 and the more satisfactory completed process in stage 5.

In relationships, however, a couple does not just arrive at this point to live happily ever after. There is a continual ebb and flow, back to stage 3, then 4, then 5, again and again. Hopefully, the process never ends. It is simply understood as natural and necessary, not fearful. While one partner needs space, trouble comes with a partner fearfully clinging, thinking this means the relationship is folding.

Let's discuss some of the common paradoxes facing married couples.

PARADOX 1: **In order to be close, there must be space.** In order to relate, there must be **two.** Therefore, the breaking down of the symbiotic tie where a couple is seen as **one,** is vitally important. The impact of stage 3 is at once painful but positive. Each partner requires an aloneness to develop a private self with which to relate. Only when one's aloneness is very clear is one free to truly share with another.

PARADOX 2: **The only way to have a relationship is to let go.**

We tend to hold on, to control, hopefully to insure that we will not lose what we value. Since a human being requires freedom, he or she will resist against domination and control by another. The quickest way to alienate another person is through attempts to control or to have it your way.

Expectations are control devices used on mates that only cause resentments and resistance. People control out of fear, not realizing that they are causing the very situation they are trying to prevent. The tighter one holds, the more the partner will struggle to be free. The decision to come closer can only be made by a person who is free. So ask for what you want from your mate, realizing all the while that a request allows for a **yes** or a **no** answer.

All growth is letting go, a taking a risk. Like breathing, we let go of the old breath which gave us life, trusting a new breath will come in. Hanging on to the old way, or to expectations, is death. So, let go, take a risk, stop controlling. Instead exercise your power and request what you want or need. You may receive it -- freely.

"If you love something, set it free.
If it returns to you, it's yours.
If not, it never was." *(anonymous)*

PARADOX 3: **You can only give to another when you have given to yourself first.** We often come to each other empty inside, expecting our partner to fill us up, to make us happy. It is an impossible task we are assigning to our spouse, since other people do not produce the feelings inside us. We produce them. Yet, we expect our spouse to do it.

The answer is to care for yourself, make yourself happy, fill your own emptiness inside and then you come to the marriage filled up with love and good feelings to share with your partner. You are filled and can share instead of being empty and trying to get filled, or completed by your spouse. We want to learn to manage our lives through love not fear.

PARADOX 4: **You cannot truly be in a marriage until you recognize the part of you that wants out.**

We have many parts or aspects of ourselves, subpersonalities, such as, the scared child, the judge, the mystic, the controller, the bitch, the workaholic, or others. These parts often conflict with each other. Each person who decides to get married and feels good and right and happy about this always has the opposite aspect inside. This part fears closeness, commitment, feels it may mean a loss of freedom. It is important to recognize and deal with this part of otherwise it will move into the unconscious part of your mind there to have free reign because you have no awareness of it, therefore, no control of it. This may result in that unconscious part working to move you out of your relationship. Whatever you are aware of you can control or deal with in some fashion and have some power over the outcome.

Each person has this part desiring freedom inside and may be recognized by beliefs such as these: "I think it would really be neat to furnish the bedroom the way **I** want. I'd like to be able to stop for a drink after work without checking with anyone. I always wanted to buy a motorcycle and take out across country. I wish I didn't have so many people I'm responsible for. If I were alone, I wouldn't cook, I'd just eat a hot dog tonight. I'd like to watch a different TV program tonight than the one we always do."

Do not be afraid to recognize this part in you. Everyone has it and it is natural. The important point here is to recognize it so that you can have control of it rather than have it controlling you, maybe pushing you right out of your marriage.

PARADOX 5: **Commitment goes hand-in-hand with freedom.**

We have seen how important freedom is to people and their successful functioning in a relationship. Freedom is valued highly by most people, even our country was founded on a need for freedom. We require freedom for our growth and sense of well-being.

However, it has been a belief that marriage means a loss of that freedom. Freedom and commitment are not mutually exclusive. You can commit yourself to a situation and still retain your freedom. Remember freedom is the ability to make choices and as long as you keep the right to choose you are free. So you can be free in a relationship. Freedom is a state of consciousness that you produce.

However, if you believe you give up your right to be free, or your right to be aware of your wants and needs and your right to ask that those needs be met, or your right to choose, you will feel trapped. If you feel you have to do "it" the way your mate wants or needs without your choice being involved, you will have essentially given up your freedom. If that has happened for you, just reactivate your conscious choice in each and every situation and begin actively choosing -- "Yes, I want this shirt. No, I don't want to go to that movie. Yes, I'd like spagetti tonight. Yes, I'd love to have sex with you." And you **will** have your fredom back. Since it is a state of consciousness, you can have it return at will.

Freedom is required inorder to make a commitment so realize the importance of being consciously aware that you are indeed free. Until you do, you will be fighting in the wrong arena against your spouse for your freedom instead of within yourself where the true loss of freedom occurs.

PARADOX 6: **You have more power when you discontinue manipulating and controlling your partner and allow freedom of choice.**

When you were growing up, Mother could neglect feeding or changing you and you were helpless to do it for yourself. Parents could spank you and put you into your bed. You had less power and you soon learned to cry, become angry, sulk, become ill, feel sorry for yourself, or be a smiling people-pleaser to get your needs met. You learned to manipulate others with your emotions.

The adult says in fear, "Well, I'll just leave if you don't do such-and-such," -- or in anger, "You s.o.b.," -- or in lack, "You never hold me anymore," -- or in people-pleasing behavior, "I just can't do it without you."

Straight-forward leveling communication methods of asking for what you want and need from your partner is direct, with each partner freely communicating and freely choosing. That is power.

PARADOX 7: **People are stronger when they allow their weaknesses to show.**

In order to arrive at a position of power and strength, paradoxically, one must acknowledge feeling insecure and afraid at times, not only strong and capable.

Men are trained in our society to deny their fearful, vulnerable parts, while women have permission to acknowledge that aspect of themselves. And yet, women were taught to deny their powerful aspects, and instead, they learned to use this strength unconsciously to manipulate.

Denial of fearful aspects of ourselves makes us feel separate from others. Friends are in a cooperative journey through life together; they support each other by loving, sharing, and resolving conflicts with problem-solving communication rather than manipulation.

PARADOX 8: **Acceptance of the mate and the relationship "as it is" is the most effective way to growth and change.**

When the battle of **Expectations vs. Acceptance** begins, the partners expect it to be as they pictured. Then all effort is directed toward this end.

Paradoxically, if each person could accept the mate as he or she actually is or accept the relationship as it is, then (and only then) is change actually possible.

Acceptance does not mean approval. Acceptance is seeing the reality of the situation -- seeing it as it is. Furthermore, nothing can be changed until it is seen as it really is, then change can be undertaken.

We expect ourselves to be perfect, then we'll be loved. We were born with inherent value and worth, however, even then we are not perfect. Don't expect perfection. Accept and love yourself, your mate, and your relationship. Acceptance allows growth. Expectations only create disappointments and power struggles.

PARADOX 9: **Awareness and expression of negative aspects is more conducive to growth than denial and repression of them.**

Most of us as children were taught to deny the negative aspects. "Don't say that, it's not nice. If you can't say something nice, don't say anything at all. I didn't hear you say hate your brother." We needed to be socialized and learn the consequences of our behavior and of our words, but this concept was carried to extremes. We began denying our negative feelings, repressing our anger and hostility, hiding our true feelings and displaying a fictional self. It seemed much safer at the time but in actuality it undermines the development of a successful relationship.

Negative feelings carefully hidden from our awareness tend to expand all out of proportion to the original incident and they will always find expression someway, somehow, sometime. Maybe in an ulcer, cancer, a fight over children, impotence in the bedroom or divorce. But the energy of those repressed feelings will come out.

It is more constructive to express the negatives at the time they occur. They are then manageable and the two of you together can deal with them, bringing peace and resolution to the relationship.

The communication methods used may need to be reworked. If you scream out your anger in "You" statements, such as, "You slob, you never pick up your socks," or "You never say you love me anymore," dealing with anger is more difficult than if you had reported, "I'm angry whenever I come in and see your socks here," or I'm afraid that your feelings for me are changing. I need to know what's going on with you now."

Therefore, expression is more functional than repression but choose the method of expressing that produces the desired results.

PARADOX 10: **The more we become aware of our differences, uniqueness and separation; the more connection and intimacy we can achieve in our relationships.**

There is a constant interplay and tension between the part of us that desires connection and intimacy and the part that must have separation and autonomy. If we know this pull of these polarities is normal, natural and human, we will not have the urge to completely get out of the marriage in order to feel autonomous, or to hang-on and be possessive in order to combat the feeling of loneliness.

The feminine nature within each person wants

connection, relatedness and to receive. Our masculine part strives for autonomy, and has an urge to give, and be responsible. We find these aspects played out in relationship struggles.

Most women have their feminine side as dominant, and will want males to come close and give to them. Prince Charming is supposed to rescue her and they will then live happily forever after.

Males will resist this because they fear being engulfed by a woman and lose their autonomy, differentness, and uniqueness. As he pulls away, she will feel alone and long for connection and intimacy.

For not only the male, but also for the female, one has to withdraw into their private self to be able to exist as a separate, distinct individual and not be enmeshed in the identity of their partner. This is a necessary part of the process of a successful relationship.

To complicate the picture we are also both spiritual and physical beings. We find the pulsating, paradoxical struggle of connection and separation going on in our physical nature. At this level it is ineffectively dealt with because we are physically separate beings and attempt to achieve a continued feeling of connection that is impossible on the physical level. The true solution is to realize that on the spiritual we are one and we can have this connection only in the spiritual realm. It has been said a solution can never be found on the same level where the problem was created because our vision is limited there. A move to a higher level provides an overview making the solution more apparent.

At the spiritual level we are all one in consciousness. This is what we are seeking: to have a consciousness of unity -- the connectedness with all life. And yet we are all individualized conscious expressions of spirit also. When we attempt to achieve this purely on the physical, we will always be disappointed and frustrated. Only when we accept the need for both separation and connection and feel the connection spiritually, can we feel satisfied on the physical level.

To become conscious of our true nature and be all that we can be is our goal here in life, and therefore to become consciously aware of this spiritual plane is an important key to a satisfying, completed relationship.

Being aware of and accepting this need for both connection and separation, for aloneness and togetherness, as a couple, you can verbally decide how each of your needs can be met so that neither of you will end up feeling trapped or disconnected.

This allows you to be connected again at a higher level of connection. It is not a compromise where each gives up some of one's self as in the self-sacrifice of marriages in the past. It is a synergy -- a synthesizing -- a higher development of each personality and then a connection on a higher level, creating a new level in the marriage.

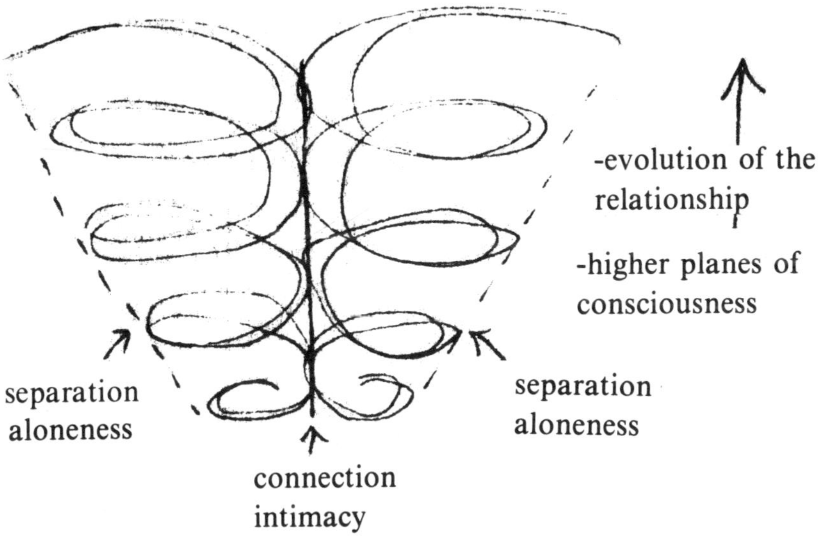

In conlusion, it becomes apparent that if we accept paradoxes as an important, inherent factor within ourselves, our relationships, and our lives, we will be benefitted. Paradoxes allow us to be aware of another perspective, eliminate the possiblity of being trapped in a position of no choice, and balance our life in a way not possible if we reject these very paradoxes that we encounter all through life.

X
PHILOSOPHICAL CONCLUSIONS FOR THE FUTURE

Marriage, like life, is a process we move through -- never remaining the same. To know and accept this idea releases us from the bondage to the impossible task of trying to "fix it up, once and for all."

If we let go and flow with the process, if we can be present and aware of where we are now, (the essence of acceptance), we can enjoy and appreciate the good that is present in this marriage and we can change what is not working. This is what life is all about -- acceptance, responsibility, choice and change.

Now for the first time on a large scale, it is possible for marriages to function at this level because the awareness of mankind has evolved out of the era of child-like helplessness and self-sacrifice into the era of responsibility, love and acceptance.

There may have been an occasional marriage long ago that operated on these principles, but now it is possible for the majority of marriages to be this way if the couple chooses to do so. They are the creators of what this marriage is uniquely to be.

As each couple succeeds in finding a new way of being together without the self-sacrifice of the past, they will be a model for other marriages. Couples today are truly the architects of the marriage of the future. Today's new woman and new man will create a new way to be married.

Human beings long for connection with one another. This is probably an aspect of the longing for oneness again with their creator. Whatever the urge truly is, it is present and unrelenting -- this movement toward unity and connectedness with life.

However, the polarity just as unrelentlessly moves each individual toward separation. Striving for balance and becoming comfortable with the pulsating force between those urges for separation and connection is a necessity for successful marriages. Being stuck in either polarity is certain death to progress.

Excitingly enough, the change in marriage relationships will positively affect all relationships, setting change into motion on this planet. We human beings hold within our power, the possibility of creating a new world of cooperation instead of conflict, acceptance instead of rejection, responsibility instead of dependency, choice instead of sacrifice, brotherly love instead of domination.

Each inroad of cooperation achieved whether between parent and child, husband and wife, friend and friend is like lighting one little candle that combined could possibly produce enough light to promote cooperation country to country and nation to nation -- maybe enlightening the world.

So take the task of creating a new way to be married seriously, like ripples in a pond, your efforts may affect changes in ways and in places you never dreamed possible.

REFERENCE LIST

Assagioli, Robert, **The Act of Will,** Penguin Books, Inc., Baltimore, Md., 1973

Bach, George, **Pairing,**

Branden, Nathaniel, **Disowned Self,** Bantam Books, N.Y., 1972

Ellis, Albert, **Growth through Reason,** Science and Behavior Books, Palo Alto, Cal. 1971

Emery, Stewart, **Actualizations,** Doubleday & Co., Inc., Garden City, N.Y. 1978

Erikson, Erik, **Childhood and Society,** W.W. Norton & Co., Inc., N.Y., N.YU. 1963

Keyes, Ken, **Handbook to Higher Consciousness,** Living Love Center, Maryland, 1975

Krantzler, Mel, **Learning to Love Again,** Thomas H. Crowell Co., N.Y.,N.Y. 1977

Kuhbler-Ross, Elizabeth, **On Death and Dying** Macmillan Publishing Co., Inc., N.Y., N.Y. 1969

Maltz, Maxwell, **Psychocybernetics,** Pocket Books, N.Y., N.Y., 1969

Maslow, Abraham, in **Theories of Personality,** Ed. Hall, Calvin S., Lindzey, Gardner, John Wiley & Sons, Inc., N.Y., 1970

O'Neill, Nena & O'Neill, George, **Open Marriage,** The Hearst Corp., New York, N.Y., 1972

Powell, John, **The Secret of Staying in Love,** Argus Communications, Niles, Ill., 1974

Rubin, T.I., **Compassion and Self Hate,** Ballentine Books, N.Y., N.Y., 1975

Satir, Virginia, **Peoplemaking,** Science & Behavior Books, Inc., Palo Alto, Cal., 1972

Schutz, William C., **The Interpersonal Underworld,** Science & Behavior Books, Inc., Palo Alto, Cal., 1966

Smith, Manuel J., **When I say No, I Feel Guilty,** Bantam Books, N.Y., N.Y., 1975

Viscott, David, **How to Live With Another Person,** Pocket Books, N.Y., N.Y., 1976